MURDERED TO DEATH

MURDERED TO DEATH

by Peter Gordon

JOSEF WEINBERGER PLAYS

LONDON

MURDERED TO DEATH
First published in 1993
by Josef Weinberger Ltd
(pka Warner/Chappell Plays Ltd)
12-14 Mortimer Street, London, W1T 3JJ

ISBN 0 85676 105 2

Printed by Commercial Colour Press plc, London E7 0EW

This revised edition of MURDERED TO DEATH was first presented by Peter Frosdick and Martin Dodd for UK Productions Ltd at the Grand Opera House, York, on September 2nd 2002, prior to a national UK tour. The cast was as follows:

MILDRED	Mary Duddy
DOROTHY	Shona Lindsay
BUNTING	Nicholas Smith
COLONEL CHARLES CRADDOCK	Geoffrey Davies
MARGARET CRADDOCK	Sarah Whitlock
ELIZABETH HARTLEY-TRUMPINGTON	Rachel Mulcahy
PIERRE MARCEAU	Andrew Loudon
JOAN MAPLE	Anna Karen
CONSTABLE THOMPKINS	Richard Elis
INSPECTOR PRATT	Trevor Bannister

Directed by Julian Woolford
Designed by Charles Camm
Lighting Design by David Howe

CHARACTERS

MILDRED

DOROTHY, *companion and housekeeper to* MILDRED

BUNTING, *the Butler*

COLONEL CHARLES CRADDOCK

MARGARET CRADDOCK, *his wife*

PIERRE MARCEAU, *a French art dealer*

ELIZABETH HARTLEY-TRUMPINGTON, *very high society*

JOAN MAPLE

INSPECTOR PRATT

CONSTABLE THOMPKINS

The action of the play takes place in the lounge of a country manor house in the 1930s.

ACT ONE

ACT TWO

ACT ONE

Scene One

The action takes place in the lounge of an old country manor house in the mid 1930s. The lounge, though tastefully decorated and furnished, is in need of re-decoration. A door centre stage leads to the hallway. Adjacent to the door is a sideboard on top of which is a telephone. Stage right, a door leads to the dining room. Downstage of the doorway is a writing desk. Stage left is a window with heavy drape curtains, adjacent to a small table on which is a lamp. Down from the table is a fireplace in which a fire is burning low. On the hearth is a carved wooden elephant and an empty scuttle for logs. The room is further furnished with a three-seater settee, four chairs and a coffee table. Two paintings hang prominently on the wall above the fireplace. It is late afternoon in autumn, and the curtains are open to reveal that it is dark outside. MILDRED *is sitting by the fire. She is in her late fifties and is the moderately wealthy owner of the house.* MILDRED'S *niece,* DOROTHY, *is sitting on the settee reading a magazine. She is in her late twenties and plainly dressed. She acts as companion and housekeeper to* MILDRED.

MILDRED	Are you absolutely sure that the dinner will be ready, Dorothy?
DOROTHY	(*wearily*) Of course. I've been in the kitchen burning it for most of the day.
MILDRED	(*not convinced*) It's so rarely that I have people for dinner these days.
DOROTHY	(*quietly to herself*) I thought you'd prefer mutton actually.
MILDRED	Pardon, dear?
DOROTHY	Sorry?
MILDRED	Sorry, I thought you spoke. (*Warming her hands at the fire.*) Would you close the curtains, dear. It seems to get so cold in here.

DOROTHY   (*slamming her magazine down*) Absolutely . . .
           I'd love to. Nothing better to do.

           (*As* DOROTHY *crosses to the window,* MILDRED
           *picks up the carved elephant from the hearth
           and throws it into the fire.* DOROTHY *notices
           her and runs to the fire.*)

           Aunty! That's the elephant!

           (DOROTHY *pulls the elephant from the fire and
           examines it.*)

MILDRED   Oh dear, how careless of me. Is it damaged?

DOROTHY   A little scorched down one side but I think it'll
           survive. You ought to start wearing your
           spectacles, then we wouldn't have these little
           accidents, would we?

           (DOROTHY *places the elephant back on the
           hearth, moves to the window and closes the
           curtains.*)

MILDRED   No, I couldn't possibly . . . they make me look
           old. I know I am getting old but at least without
           the spectacles I can't see that I am. Colonel
           Craddock gave me the elephant you know. A
           present from India.

DOROTHY   (*returning to* MILDRED) They're meant to be
           unlucky when they have their trunks raised.
           That one was nearly very unlucky. There aren't
           any logs left. I'll send Bunting in . . . if I can
           find him.

MILDRED   What do you mean, dear?

DOROTHY   He gives me the shivers. Creeping around the
           place . . . lurking in dark corners. I never know
           where he's going to leap out from next!

MILDRED Don't exaggerate, Dorothy. Bunting never leaps . . . he's not capable of it.

DOROTHY Well, he definitely lurks. I can't understand why you keep him on, He's hopeless!

(DOROTHY *exits to the hall.* MILDRED *does not realise that* DOROTHY *has left and continues talking.*)

MILDRED Bunting? Why, I couldn't possibly let him go . . . he's practically an institution here. Oh, it's going to be marvellous having a house full of guests again . . . like the old days. It must be nearly two years since we were all together in Paris. Do you remember that holiday? Happy days.

(*As* MILDRED *continues,* BUNTING *enters slowly from the hall. He is in his sixties and is dressed as a traditional butler. He wears white gloves. He moves menacingly towards* MILDRED, *carrying a log in one hand and a raised axe in the other hand.*)

I'm so looking forward to seeing the Colonel again. And Pierre. Such a charming young man . . . he made me feel years younger. Perhaps it was just the Paris air. (*Shivering.*) Do hurry up and fetch Bunting, dear.

(BUNTING *is now alongside though slightly behind* MILDRED. *His speech is slow and measured.*)

BUNTING (*loud and without warning*) Logs, Ma'am.

MILDRED (*with a shriek, startled*) Oh, Bunting! I do wish you'd announce yourself at the door. And put that axe down . . . you look like a mad man.

BUNTING (*sarcastically*) I can't chop logs without it, Ma'am. I'm not an exponent of the martial arts.

MILDRED	(*controlling her anger*) But there's no need to bring it in here. Put a log on the fire and leave the rest by the side.
BUNTING	I only brought the one, Ma'am. It was rather heavy.
MILDRED	(*sighing*) Really, Bunting, I don't know why I bother!
BUNTING	I didn't realise you did, Ma'am.

(MILDRED *scowls at* BUNTING *who remains impassive.*)

MILDRED	Just put the log on the fire, Bunting.
BUNTING	Very good, Ma'am.

(BUNTING *throws the log casually onto the fire without moving.* MILDRED *glares at him.*)

Will there be anything else, Ma'am?

MILDRED	I expect that the guests will be arriving shortly. I suggest that you station yourself by the front door so they don't have to wait for ten minutes.
BUNTING	By the front door, Ma'am. As you like.

(BUNTING *turns and moves slowly to the hall door.*)

MILDRED	And we'll be wanting sherry when they've all arrived.
BUNTING	Sherry, Ma'am. As you like. (*Turning at the door.*) Will that be the best sherry, Ma'am, or the cooking?
MILDRED	(*standing*) Really, Bunting, the best of course!

BUNTING	I only ask, Ma'am, because there is very little of the best left. Half a bottle.
MILDRED	What! But we only recently re-stocked!
BUNTING	You must have drunk it, Ma'am.
MILDRED	What! What did you say, Bunting?
BUNTING	I said you must have drunk it, Ma'am.
MILDRED	(*angry*) Now look here, Bunting . . . I think it's time you were reminded of your position in this house!
BUNTING	I know my position, Ma'am. I'm in the lounge at the present time.
MILDRED	Bunting, will you please stop answering back!
BUNTING	I'll try to curb my naturally exuberant nature, Ma'am. Will that be all?
MILDRED	Yes it will. Re-order more sherry next week.
BUNTING	Very good, Ma'am . . . as you like.

(BUNTING *exits slowly to the hall, turning left as he exits. He leaves the door open.*)

| MILDRED | Door, Bunting. |

(MILDRED *receives no response, sighs heavily and sits as* DOROTHY *enters from the dining room.*)

I think you're right about Bunting. He's becoming insufferable.

| DOROTHY | I found him trying to chop logs in the kitchen. I ask you . . . with all that food around! |

(MILDRED *looks at* DOROTHY *anxiously.*)

Oh, don't worry, he rarely manages to hit anything.

MILDRED   Well I think we need to keep a close eye on him. He's started on the sherry again.

DOROTHY   Oh no! I thought we'd weaned him off that after the last episode.

MILDRED   Well, if he goes missing again, at least we'll know where to find him.

DOROTHY   You'd think a man of his age would have more sense. He could have died of exposure in that fish pond. Incidentally, I heard some gossip about him in the village. He's been telling someone in the pub about his lurid past. An affair he had with a woman years ago.

MILDRED   Bunting . . . an affair! It seems highly unlikely to me. I mean, who would want him!

(*A door bell rings, off.*)

Ah, at last. I thought they were never going to arrive.

DOROTHY   Shall I get it?

MILDRED   No. Bunting can earn his keep for once.

(BUNTING *passes the open door, shuffling down the hall at full speed towards the front door.* MILDRED *rises, patting her hair with her hand.*)

Do I look presentable, dear?

DOROTHY   Don't worry, you look fine. Just sit back and enjoy the weekend with your friends.

MILDRED   Thank you for organising everything, Dorothy. I don't know how I'd manage without you.

(BUNTING *appears at the hall door. He holds up a hand to stop the guests following him and they remain out of sight. He takes a step into the room.*)

BUNTING   Bunting, Ma'am.

MILDRED   What do you mean? Where are the guests!

BUNTING   You instructed me to announce myself at all times, Ma'am.

MILDRED   Not when there are guests to announce! Let them in immediately.

BUNTING   As you like, Ma'am.

(BUNTING *casually gestures with his head for the guests to enter.* MARGARET *and* COLONEL CHARLES CRADDOCK *enter, practically bundling* BUNTING *out of the way.* CHARLES *is in his early sixties. Dressed in tweeds, he has a confident but blustering manner.* MARGARET *is somewhat younger than* CHARLES.)

MARGARET   (*as she passes* BUNTING) Thank you, Bunting. Mildred, how nice to see you again.

(MARGARET *crosses to* MILDRED *and greets her with two extravagant 'air' kisses.*)

CHARLES   Mildred, old girl. How are you, m'dear? Let's have a look at you. By Jove, you look younger every time I see you.

(CHARLES *gives* MILDRED *a kiss on the cheek.*)

MILDRED   Charles, really!

(CHARLES *turns to* DOROTHY.)

CHARLES   And how's young, Dorothy? Still keeping an eye on the old battle-axe, eh? Marvellous.

BUNTING	Colonel and Missus Craddock, Ma'am.
MILDRED	Pardon, Bunting?
BUNTING	I said, Colonel and Missus Craddock, Ma'am.
MILDRED	Bunting, you announce guests as they enter . . . not five minutes later.
BUNTING	They didn't give me the chance, Ma'am. Will that be all?
MILDRED	(*controlling her anger*) Yes, Bunting . . . thank you. Take the bags up to the green bedroom would you?
BUNTING	The green bedroom. As you like, Ma'am. I expect I'll manage them by myself somehow.
MILDRED	And more guests should be arriving shortly.
BUNTING	How very delightful for you, Ma'am. I expect you'll be wanting me to position myself by the front door again, so they don't have to wait.
	(BUNTING *exits to the hall, turning right. He leaves the door open.*)
MILDRED	(*calling after him*) Door, Bunting. (*Receiving no response.*) I'm afraid you'll have to forgive Bunting. He's not quite himself these days.
CHARLES	Bunting . . . Bunting. Sure I've seen him somewhere . . . never forget a chap's face.
MARGARET	Of course you've seen him before, Charles. You've been *here* before.
CHARLES	Have I? Yes, course I have. Peculiar feller though.
MILDRED	Of course, this is your first visit here, Margaret.

MARGARET	And I must say that I'm very impressed. The grounds seem to be huge.
MILDRED	Seven acres. Of course the estate is several thousand acres but it's all leased out to local farmers these days. Do sit, please.
	(*They all sit with the exception of* CHARLES.)
	Charles?
CHARLES	What? Sorry, miles away. Still trying to place that queer feller. Never forget a face. Only the other day, saw a chap I hadn't come across for years. Recognised him at once. "Why, Beaky, old boy", I said, "How're you keeping". Chap was absolutely amazed.
DOROTHY	That you recognised him?
CHARLES	What? Good Lord, no. Said he'd never seen me before in his life. Got quite abusive . . . seemed to object to being called Beaky. Bit of an odd chap as it turned out.
MARGARET	(*bored*) You're not going to bore us with pointless stories all weekend, Charles?
CHARLES	Sorry, old girl. Just a spot of fun.
MILDRED	He wouldn't be the same old Charles without his little stories. I find them rather amusing.
MARGARET	(*caustic*) But you don't hear them as often as I.
	(*There is an awkward silence.*)
MILDRED	Would either of you care for a sherry?
MARGARET	Not for me, thank you.
CHARLES	You know me . . . ready for a snifter any time. Long as the sun's over the yard arm of course.

MILDRED   Dorothy, dear, would you call Bunting.

DOROTHY   (*standing*) It's all right, Aunty, I don't think he could cope with any more jobs at the moment.

(DOROTHY *exits to the dining room.*)

CHARLES   Delightful young gal. If I were thirty years younger!

MARGARET   (*caustic*) But you're not, Charles. (*To* MILDRED.) It must be rather nice for you, having a young person about the house.

MILDRED   Yes it is. (*Smiling.*) I don't know how she puts up with me sometimes, I get so irritable these days.

CHARLES   (*cheerfully*) Old age . . . comes to us all. Take Margaret here.

(MARGARET *glares at him.*)

Just a bit of a joke, old girl.

MILDRED   I really am very grateful to Dorothy. I sometimes think she should be socialising with people of her own age but, as I keep telling her, there's no one suitable around here. One has to be so careful not to lower one's standards. Still, if she continues to follow my advice she'll be very well rewarded.

MARGARET   Really?

MILDRED   None of us live forever. When I'm gone, Dorothy will benefit most handsomely . . . I have no other relatives now.

MARGARET   But I thought . . . (*Hurriedly.*) I thought you had other relatives.

MILDRED   None at all. I've seen them all off. Dorothy was so young when her parents died. Tragic circumstances. My sister's fault for taking up with the wrong sort. He drank and gambled away most of her fortune and squandered all of the rest. They ended up penniless and hating each other.

MARGARET   It sounds terrible. How did they die?

MILDRED   A suicide pact. They killed each other.

MARGARET   How dreadful!

MILDRED   Actually, more of a murder pact. He hacked her head off with their last remaining decent piece of silver . . . an attractive but rather blunt fish knife. Ironically, he, himself, died the following day. It transpired that she'd been slowly poisoning him for months. I sometimes think that Dorothy holds me to blame because I'd always refused to settle their debts.

CHARLES   Come on now . . . all this morbid talk's getting me depressed! Did I ever tell you about the time that . . .

(DOROTHY *enters with a silver tray on which are a sherry decanter and several glasses.*)

DOROTHY   Sorry it took so long . . . Bunting had hidden it.

(*She goes to the sideboard and pours drinks for* MILDRED *and* CHARLES.)

CHARLES   Still can't place the chap. Damned irritating.

MILDRED   I shouldn't let it worry you, Charles. You were about to tell us one of your stories.

(DOROTHY *hands out the drinks.*)

CHARLES   Was I? Don't suppose you recollect what it was about . . . dashed if I can remember. Still, it'll come to me later. Anyway, here's to us all . . . very best of health.

(CHARLES *drinks the sherry in one gulp, then looks at the empty glass.*)

Don't seem to make sherry glasses so large these days!

MILDRED   (*smiling*) Help yourself, Charles.

CHARLES   What? I wasn't suggesting . . . still, if you insist.

(CHARLES *moves to pour himself another drink as* MARGARET *stands.*)

MARGARET   If you'll excuse me, Mildred, I'd like to freshen up. It's such an exhausting drive down here . . . especially with Charles at the wheel.

DOROTHY   I'll show you to your room, Missus Craddock.

MARGARET   No, there's no need to trouble yourself, dear. I'll ask Bunting. Excuse me.

(MARGARET *exits to the hall, closing the door as she leaves.*)

MILDRED   You've still got the old banger then, Charles?

CHARLES   What, Margaret! Yes, afraid so.

MILDRED   I meant the car.

CHARLES   Oh, see what you mean. That's not a banger, it's a Bentley. Wouldn't be without her. Mind you, take your point . . . she is getting a bit temperamental in her old age. Still, so's Margaret come to that.

DOROTHY   (*moving to the dining room door*) I'd better check the dinner. Is there anything else you want, Aunty?

MILDRED   No thank you, dear.

(DOROTHY *exits.* MILDRED *stands.*)

Well, Charles, how have you been?

CHARLES	(*awkwardly*) Oh, not bad y'know. Lot's of stick from Margaret. Seems to think I spend too much time at the club. Can't understand her . . . chap needs the company of other chaps. Know where you stand with chaps.
MILDRED	Stop rambling, Charles, you know what I mean. (*Advancing on* CHARLES.) When are you going to take me up on my little proposition?
CHARLES	(*retreating from her*) Steady, old girl. You're putting me in a dashed awkward spot.
MILDRED	Do you remember, Charles, thirty years ago?
CHARLES	Course I do, as though it were yesterday. Nineteen hundred and six . . . Kent won the County Championship.
MILDRED	The year we met . . . when our affair started.
CHARLES	(*clearing his throat, uncomfortable*) Ah that . . . hmn . . . yes. Damned long time ago. Lot of water under the bridge and all that.
MILDRED	And ever since, you've been promising, Charles. Next year . . . then the year after that.
CHARLES	We're getting too long in the tooth for all that sort of stuff now, old girl. Chap tends to slow down a bit.
MILDRED	(*advancing to* CHARLES *again*) I don't expect it still to be a mad passionate thing, Charles. All I want is you. Your company, your companionship. I'm not asking for the world. I just want you here . . . with me.

CHARLES　　　But what about Margaret? I can't let the old
　　　　　　　girl down . . . not after all these years.

MILDRED　　　You've never loved each other. Not as we did
　　　　　　　. . . not as we still do. We should have taken
　　　　　　　the plunge years ago.

CHARLES　　　But that's just the point, old girl. We've left it
　　　　　　　too late. Yes, there was a time after your Albert
　　　　　　　died that we might have made a go of it, but
　　　　　　　not now. We're too set in our ways. Margaret
　　　　　　　depends on me too much.

MILDRED　　　You're wrong, Charles. You belong here with
　　　　　　　me. I'll never let you go until the day that I die.

CHARLES　　　Dash it all, Mildred. It's got to stop. All these
　　　　　　　letters you keep sending me at the club.
　　　　　　　Damned embarrassing for a chap when his mail
　　　　　　　stinks of perfume . . . other chaps are starting
　　　　　　　to talk. Bad form . . . won't do . . . got to end.

MILDRED　　　No, Charles, it won't end. You're all I've got
　　　　　　　left. (*Scheming.*) What if I were to tell Margaret
　　　　　　　about us?

CHARLES　　　Mildred! You wouldn't do that . . . would you?

MILDRED　　　It's time she knew . . . this weekend.

CHARLES　　　Mildred, old girl, think what you're saying.

　　　　　　　(DOROTHY *enters from the dining room and
　　　　　　　immediately notices the tension.*)

DOROTHY　　　Oh, I'm sorry. I didn't mean to barge in. Would
　　　　　　　you rather . . .

MILDRED　　　No, come on in, Dorothy. I was just telling
　　　　　　　Charles that Margaret ought to know.

CHARLES　　　Mildred!

　　　　　　　(CHARLES *refills his sherry glass hurriedly.*)

MILDRED	I think she'd be amused, don't you, Charles?

(CHARLES *looks at* MILDRED *in sheer panic and gulps the sherry in one.*)

About my little accident with the elephant.

CHARLES	What? (*Confused.*) Oh, yes, of course.
DOROTHY	Oh that. I rescued her just in time. There'd have been a terrible mess.
CHARLES	(*even more confused*) Yes, expect there would . . . tricky beasts . . . came across a lot in India y'know.

(*The door bell rings.*)

MILDRED	Ah, another guest.
DOROTHY	I'll go. I think Bunting's still upstairs. Short of sliding down the banister it'll take him ages!
MILDRED	No, dear. You do too much running around. I'll go myself. I won't be a moment, Charles.

(MILDRED *exits to the hall.* CHARLES *is still rather flustered.*)

DOROTHY	Are you all right, Colonel? You look rather pale.
CHARLES	What? Ah. No, just a spot of mental indigestion . . . bit of a problem cropped up. Still, nothing we can't put right. (*Recovering.*) Other guests . . . do I know 'em?
DOROTHY	You certainly do. They were in Paris. Pierre Marceau and (*With a false sophisticated accent.*) Elizabeth Hartley-Trumpington.
CHARLES	(*thinking*) Marceau . . . Marceau. No recollection whatsoever. Foreign chap is he?

DOROTHY	He's French. Don't you remember Elizabeth either?
CHARLES	Ah, now, that's a different matter. Pretty young gal.
DOROTHY	(*bitterly*) That's her.
CHARLES	(*cheering considerably*) Rather well endowed as I recall.

(DOROTHY *glances at* CHARLES *in surprise.*)

Hmn. In the financial sense of course . . . enormous assets.

(MILDRED *enters, followed by* ELIZABETH *and* PIERRE. ELIZABETH *is in her mid-twenties, attractive, stunningly dressed and speaks with an exaggerated high society accent. She wears white gloves.* PIERRE *is in his early thirties and speaks with a rather exaggerated French accent.*)

MILDRED	You remember Dorothy and the Colonel?
ELIZABETH	(*ignoring* DOROTHY) Colonel Craddock . . . how absolutely super to see you again. What a wonderful little lounge, Missus Bagshot . . . so quaint.
MILDRED	(*uncertain how to react*) Thank you, Elizabeth. I wasn't expecting you and Pierre to arrive together.
ELIZABETH	Tremendous stroke of luck. I'd just settled on the train with a boring old book when Pierre got into the very same compartment.
PIERRE	I 'ave the 'appy knack of finding myself always in the company of beautiful women.

ELIZABETH	(*giggling*) He's been talking like that all the way. It certainly brightened up the journey . . . (*Distasteful.*) . . . so tedious passing through all those horrid industrial areas where the working people live . . . quite ghastly.
CHARLES	Chap's quite right of course. Got an eye for a pretty young gal myself.
ELIZABETH	One tries one's best to look presentable.
DOROTHY	I expect one has to.
ELIZABETH	Why, Dorothy darling, I hadn't noticed you there. And how nice . . . you're wearing that lovely little frock I so admired in Paris all that time ago!
MILDRED	(*hastily*) Do sit down, everyone. Would anyone care for a sherry?
	(*They all sit.*)
CHARLES	Wouldn't say no old girl.
MILDRED	Dorothy, would you be so kind?
	(DOROTHY *moves to the sideboard and pours drinks.*)
CHARLES	What brings you over here Mister . . . er . . . hmn . . . old chap?
MILDRED	Surely you remember, Charles, Pierre's a painter.
CHARLES	Oh, yes . . . course. (*Glancing around the room.*) Thought the old place looked in need of a coat or two.
MILDRED	Charles!
CHARLES	(*oblivious*) What?

PIERRE   I come to sell some paintings I 'ope. I stay for two or three weeks, depending on my success.

CHARLES   Ah . . . right, get your meaning.

ELIZABETH   The man's an absolute genius . . . absolutely super.

PIERRE   You flatter me, Elizabeth. Unfortunately I 'ave to make my money in other peoples work. 'Ow you say . . . a dealer wheeler.

(DOROTHY *hands out drinks.*)

ELIZABETH   I really don't know how he can drag himself away from Paris. Super little town.

CHARLES   Passable. Don't care much for that enormous iron erection. Damned civilised licensing hours of course.

ELIZABETH   And the fashions. I have to travel to Paris at least twice a year for the fashions. One can't go around in rags . . . (*Looking pointedly at* DOROTHY.) . . . can one, Dorothy?

CHARLES   Fashions? Can't see the fuss. All a waste of time if you ask me.

PIERRE   But, Colonel, if you will forgive me, that is the trouble with you British. No daring . . . no sense of adventure.

CHARLES   (*bristling*) No lack of daring in the British, old boy. Agincourt . . . Waterloo . . . get my point? No use you chaps wearing fancy hats if you keep getting 'em shot off.

MILDRED   Please, Charles, let's not fall out.

CHARLES   Just making a point.

PIERRE   I am sorry, I 'ave offended you. I withdraw my words.

CHARLES	Tactical retreat, eh? Now there's a thing you chaps are good at.

(BUNTING *enters at the hall door.*)

BUNTING	Bunting, Ma'am.
MILDRED	Yes, Bunting, what is it?
BUNTING	I wonder if I might have a word, Ma'am.
MILDRED	Carry on.
BUNTING	As you like, Ma'am.

(BUNTING *goes to exit.*)

MILDRED	Where are you going?
BUNTING	To carry on, Ma'am . . . as you instructed.
MILDRED	(*trying to be patient*) I meant carry on and tell me.
BUNTING	I see, Ma'am. I thought you meant for me to carry on with my duties. You usually tell me to carry on when you want me to carry on.
MILDRED	(*exasperated*) What did you want to tell me?
BUNTING	It's just about the accident, Ma'am.
MILDRED	Accident!
BUNTING	In the kitchen, Ma'am. A small mishappening with the axe. The head fell off . . . at some speed, Ma'am.
DOROTHY	I'll come and have a look in a moment, Bunting.
BUNTING	As you like.

(MILDRED *carries on, expecting* BUNTING *to leave, but he remains at the door.*)

MILDRED I think we should make plans for the weekend. Any suggestions?

CHARLES Thought I might get a spot of shooting in. Damned good sport around here if I remember. Don't suppose you shoot do you, Mister er . . . old boy?

PIERRE I prefer to create rather than destroy. I would not know one end of a gun from the other.

CHARLES Ah well, never mind old chap . . . you are French . . . quite understandable.

(BUNTING *clears his throat loudly.* MILDRED *is surprised to see him still at the door.*)

MILDRED Yes, Bunting, was there something else?

BUNTING I was wondering if you might want me to take any action in the meantime.

MILDRED What about?

BUNTING The fire, Ma'am.

MILDRED (*glancing at the fire*) It's all right for the moment, Bunting. You can bring more logs in later.

BUNTING I meant the fire in the kitchen, Ma'am.

MILDRED We haven't got a fire in the kitchen.

BUNTING We have now, Ma'am.

MILDRED What!

BUNTING It's just a small one, Ma'am . . . at present . . . on the stove. Although the dinner is starting to look somewhat over cooked.

DOROTHY	(*shrieking*) The food!
	(DOROTHY *rushes out to the dining room*.)
MILDRED	Don't just stand there, Bunting . . . help!
BUNTING	As you like, Ma'am.
	(BUNTING *exits, shuffling away in to the dining room*.)
MILDRED	I knew something was going to go wrong today . . . I just knew.
CHARLES	Don't worry, old girl. Sure everything will turn out ship shape. Extraordinary chap you've got there. Was going to borrow him for the shoot but got second thoughts now . . . damned liability.
ELIZABETH	I wonder if I might be allowed to accompany you, Colonel? I've always wanted to try my hand, but Daddy says it's far too dangerous for a girl.
CHARLES	Quite welcome, my dear. No danger if you know what you're up to. Make an early start, eh . . . reveille at O-six hundred.
ELIZABETH	You can't possibly mean six o'clock in the morning!
CHARLES	Course I do . . . early bird and all that sort of business. You'll need stout shoes and old clothes.
ELIZABETH	Oh, how ghastly. I don't have anything like that.
MILDRED	I'm sure Dorothy will be able to lend you something.

ELIZABETH   (*smiling*) Yes, I'm sure she will. I hope no
              one's going to see me.

CHARLES   If they do we'll just have to shoot 'em. Dead
              men don't tell tales. Fancy a stroll now, before
              dinner . . . recce the ground?

MILDRED   What a good idea. What about you, Pierre?

PIERRE   If you will excuse me, I will stay 'ere. I am
              rather tired after my travels.

MILDRED   Are you sure?

PIERRE   Do not concern yourself for me. I will be very
              'appy 'ere.

CHARLES   (*standing*) Come on, Mildred, can't force the
              chap. (*Reluctantly.*) Suppose we'd better see if
              Margaret wants to come with us.

MILDRED   Very well. We shan't be long, Pierre. Help
              yourself to a drink.

              (ELIZABETH, MILDRED *and* CHARLES *exit to the
              hall.* PIERRE *waits until they have exited,
              moves to the sideboard to pour himself a
              drink, then stands looking at the paintings
              with a self satisfied grin on his face.* DOROTHY
              enters from the dining room.)

DOROTHY   Where is everyone?

PIERRE   They are taking a walk. 'Ave you repaired the
              dinner?

DOROTHY   Yes. It's not quite the same as it was, but
              nobody will notice the difference. Just taking a
              leaf out of your book.

PIERRE   (*puzzled*) I 'ave no book.

DOROTHY   No, but you were admiring your paintings.

PIERRE   I was admiring them, yes, but they are not
                mine. Such finesse. I wish I 'ad a talent to paint
                so well.

DOROTHY   I think you're far too modest. The work of a
                famous French painter you said, when you sold
                them to my aunt.

PIERRE   But of course. One day they will be worth many
                times the price that your aunt paid.

DOROTHY   (coolly) I'm sure the originals will. Such a pity
                that these are forgeries.

PIERRE   (shocked) What are you saying! You were with
                your aunt when she purchased them . . . we 'ad
                them valued by another gallery.

DOROTHY   But then you replaced the originals with your
                forgeries. You knew my aunt was ignorant
                about art . . . she'd never know the difference.

PIERRE   Dorothy, never 'ave I 'eard such a cock and
                cow story! Elizabeth can vouch for me . . .
                many times 'ave I dealt with 'er father.

DOROTHY   I don't care tuppence for how you've swindled
                Elizabeth or her father. Do you think I'm a fool,
                Pierre? I may not know about art but I do have
                a very good eye for detail.

PIERRE   You are making a very big mistake, Dorothy. I
                swear to you that these are originals.

DOROTHY   (moving to the phone) In that case, you won't
                mind if I call the police.

                (DOROTHY picks up the phone.)

PIERRE   But you are wasting your time! You will make
                yourself look very foolish, Dorothy. Your aunt
                will never forgive you.

DOROTHY   I'll just have to risk that.

(DOROTHY *tries to get a connection on the phone.* PIERRE *waits for several seconds then finally breaks.*)

PIERRE (*urgent*) Wait! Please . . . put the phone down. Per'aps we should talk a little more.

(DOROTHY *looks at him for several seconds then slowly and triumphantly replaces the phone.*)

DOROTHY So I am right? Good. I wasn't quite sure.

(PIERRE *looks devastated.*)

Take my advice, Pierre . . . never play poker . . . you'd lose very badly.

PIERRE (*pitifully*) So, you 'ave tricked me. What 'appens now?

DOROTHY (*enjoying his discomfort*) That rather depends on you. I'm not a vindictive person. Let's assume this is your first offence.

PIERRE But it is . . . I swear.

DOROTHY Well, you shouldn't . . . it's a very bad habit. My aunt paid you how much . . . two thousand pounds?

PIERRE As a favour I give her a special price of one thousand nine 'undred.

DOROTHY You're all heart. I suppose for five thousand pounds I could have a lapse of memory about this conversation.

PIERRE Five thousand! I do not 'ave five thousand!

DOROTHY Oh dear. But I don't want to cause you embarrassment, Pierre. As you were so generous I'll give you a special discount . . .

four thousand nine hundred. You have a week
. . . then I call the police.

PIERRE   But that is impossible. A week is far too short.

DOROTHY   Well, that's all you've got. You're lucky,
              Pierre. If my aunt ever found out, she wouldn't
              be so understanding.

              (MILDRED *enters from the hall.*)

MILDRED   We've abandoned all thoughts of a walk. It's
              so cold out there now.

DOROTHY   I think Pierre has been finding it rather hot in
              here.

MILDRED   Really? Remove your jacket if you wish . . .
              there's no need for ceremony amongst friends.
              The others have gone to change for dinner.
              (*Anxious.*) The dinner is all right, Dorothy?

DOROTHY   It's going to be fine.

              (MILDRED *moves to the fire to warm her hands.
              As she does so, she admires the paintings.*)

MILDRED   You'll have seen that the paintings have pride
              of place, Pierre. They do so cheer up the room.

PIERRE   (*miserable*) Ah yes . . . the paintings.

MILDRED   I'm so pleased you persuaded me to invest. I
              know I've only had them a short time, but how
              much would you say they're worth now?

DOROTHY   (*enjoying herself*) About two years I expect.

              (PIERRE *winces.*)

MILDRED   Pardon, dear?

DOROTHY   I said you've had them about two years. Well,
              Pierre . . . how much?

PIERRE	It is very difficult . . . (*Directly to* DOROTHY.) . . . almost five thousand pounds I would say.
MILDRED	Really . . . that much! You see, Dorothy, I knew I had a bargain. (*To* PIERRE.) She's never really liked them.
DOROTHY	No . . . but I'm beginning to see their good points now.
MILDRED	And how many paintings have you brought for me to look at this time, Pierre?
PIERRE	I am afraid I 'ave none for you.
MILDRED	But surely . . . your luggage in the hall?
PIERRE	My regrets but they are not suitable for you . . . (*Thinking quickly.*) . . . they are already sold.
DOROTHY	(*mischievous*) Not to any one I know?
PIERRE	Thankfully, Dorothy, no.
DOROTHY	Oh . . . what a pity.
	(MILDRED *looks puzzled by the exchange but is distracted by the door bell ringing.*)
MILDRED	Now who can that be? I'm not expecting any more visitors.
DOROTHY	Shall I go?
MILDRED	No, leave it to Bunting. It's time he earned his keep. I'm definitely starting to have reservations about him.
DOROTHY	You should have seen the state of the kitchen. It looked as though a battle had been fought in there!
	(BUNTING *enters from the hall.*)

BUNTING	Bunting, Ma'am.
MILDRED	Yes, Bunting, who is it?
BUNTING	Bunting, Ma'am. I just told you.
MILDRED	Who's at the front door?
BUNTING	Miss Maple, Ma'am. I observed her approach through the conservatory window.
MILDRED	You mean you haven't opened the door yet?
BUNTING	I thought you may wish to ignore her, Ma'am. I've heard you remark on occasion that she's an interfering busybody.
MILDRED	Bunting, really!

(*The door bell rings again.*)

(*rather reluctantly*) You'd better show her in.

BUNTING	As you like.

(BUNTING *exits to the hall.* MILDRED *and* DOROTHY *both look downcast.*)

DOROTHY	We could have ignored her. She might have gone away.
MILDRED	We couldn't do that . . . she means very well. (*To* PIERRE.) She lives down in the village . . . when she's actually there. She's always going off on holidays and visits. The curious thing is that, wherever she goes, the most dreadful things seem to happen. Someone always seems to get murdered!
DOROTHY	They positively drop like flies. She's become quite famous for it.

PIERRE   (*to* DOROTHY) In that case we will all 'ave to be very careful, Dorothy.

(BUNTING *appears at the hall door.*)

BUNTING   Bunting, Ma'am.

MILDRED   Just get on with it, Bunting.

BUNTING   As you like. Miss Maple, Ma'am.

(JOAN MAPLE *enters. She is in her sixties.* BUNTING *exits.*)

JOAN   Thank you, Mister Bunting. I hope you don't mind me calling in, Mildred? I didn't realise you had visitors.

MILDRED   That's all right, Joan. You didn't notice Colonel Craddock's car in the drive?

JOAN   A car? (*Absently.*) Oh, yes . . . yes I did. (*To* PIERRE.) I'm very pleased to meet you, Colonel.

MILDRED   No, Joan . . . this is Pierre Marceau. Another one of my guests.

JOAN   Oh, I see. How silly of me. How very nice to meet you Monsieur.

PIERRE   Enchante. I am very 'appy to meet you also. But if you will excuse me I must prepare myself for dinner.

DOROTHY   That makes you sound like a turkey, Pierre . . . waiting to be stuffed.

(MILDRED *glances sharply at* DOROTHY.)

PIERRE   Excuse me, ladies.

(PIERRE *exits.*)

JOAN	What a delightful young man. His accent rather reminds me of a Belgian gentleman I know. You have several guests staying, Mildred?
MILDRED	Yes, just a few friends . . . for the weekend.
JOAN	How charming. I do so love a party. And I can't help noticing that delicious smell emanating from the kitchen. I expect you've excelled yourself, Dorothy.
DOROTHY	Thank you, Miss Maple. It's very kind of you.
JOAN	But, I mustn't keep you. You'll want to enjoy yourself with your friends. I have a very small cold collation prepared for myself. I was hoping that my nephew would be dropping by to see me, but it seems he's rather tied up with one of his young gentleman friends. I find it so dull eating alone.
	(JOAN *waits for her hint to be taken, but with no success.*)
	Anyway, I must leave. I only called because I thought Dorothy may be away this weekend. I hated to think of you on your own up here, Mildred. (*Pause.*) Still, I have my cold collation.
MILDRED	(*guilty*) There's no need for you to leave straight away, Joan. Stay for a little while.
JOAN	No, I couldn't possibly disturb you. I expect you'll be dining soon.
MILDRED	Yes, but it's no trouble.
JOAN	I'd hate to intrude.
MILDRED	You wouldn't be.
JOAN	(*pause*) Oh, very well then, as you're so insistent. (*Sitting.*) I promise you that I have

the appetite of a sparrow . . . you'll hardly notice I'm here.

MILDRED   You're staying for dinner?

JOAN   It would be quite churlish of me to refuse such a delightful invitation.

DOROTHY   (*annoyed*) We'll be eating in thirty minutes. If you'll excuse me.

(DOROTHY *exits to the dining room.*)

JOAN   A delightful young girl. So reminds me of myself when I was that age . . . quite charming. If I remember correctly, you purchased your paintings from Pierre Marceau?

MILDRED   And never regretted it.

JOAN   I do so love art.

(CHARLES *enters from the hall.*)

CHARLES   Damned funny thing just happened. (*Noticing* JOAN.) Ah . . . excuse me, old girl . . . didn't realise you'd got company.

MILDRED   That's all right, Charles. This is Miss Maple from the village . . . Colonel Charles Craddock.

JOAN   Delighted, Colonel.

CHARLES   My pleasure, Miss, er . . . hmn.

MILDRED   We were just discussing the paintings, Charles.

CHARLES   What paintings, old girl?

MILDRED   The ones I bought from, Pierre. But of course you've never seen them have you? You left Paris before Pierre showed us his collection.

CHARLES   What . . . yes, suppose I must have.

| MILDRED | In that case, you must give me your opinion. (*To* JOAN.) Charles regards himself as something of an expert. |
| CHARLES | I've never said that, Mildred. Never been able to afford much myself. Bought the odd one for the club mind. Let's have a look. |

(*Unseen by the others*, PIERRE *is about to enter the room from the hall. Seeing* CHARLES *looking at the paintings, he remains out of sight to them at the doorway.*)

MILDRED	Well?
CHARLES	Not bad, old girl . . . not bad at all. Seen this chaps work before. Quite passable . . . damned good copies.
MILDRED	Copies!
CHARLES	Yes, of course. You did know?
MILDRED	Know? Yes of course I did.

(PIERRE *hurries away from the door.*)

JOAN	You were saying that something funny had happened, Colonel?
CHARLES	Was I? Hmn . . . so I was. Dashed funny. When we called off the walk I brought my twelve bore and my old service revolver down stairs for young Elizabeth to inspect. Twelve bore's still there but the revolver's gone missing!
JOAN	Oh dear, how inconvenient.
CHARLES	Inconvenient! Damned dangerous if you ask me . . . blighter was loaded. Could cause a serious accident.

JOAN   Perhaps it was one of the other guests playing a small joke on you, Colonel.

CHARLES   Maybe. Don't see the funny side. Damned irresponsible meddling with a chap's private things . . . could go off any time. Hmn . . . not cricket.

JOAN   Certainly not. Such a relaxing game though . . . my nephew's rather good. His friends tell me that he's a bit of a left arm bender. (*Slightly doubting.*) At least, I believe they were talking about cricket.

CHARLES   (*equally doubtful*) Yes, bound to be. Spinner. Used to bowl the odd googly m'self. Anyway, must dash . . . things to do.

     (CHARLES *exits, leaving the hall door slightly ajar.*)

JOAN   How very disturbing for the Colonel. Have you known him a very long time?

     (MILDRED *is lost in her own thoughts.*)

     Mildred?

MILDRED   I'm sorry, you said something?

JOAN   I was asking about the Colonel. How long have you known him?

MILDRED   Oh, it seems like forever. Will you excuse me a moment.

     (MILDRED *picks up her spectacles from the table and looks at the paintings briefly.*)

     I had a book somewhere . . . in the dining room I think.

     (MILDRED *crosses into the dining room.*)

JOAN   (*shouting after her*) I expect he cut a dashing
                figure in his younger days.

                (*A revolver barrel appears at the hall door,
                pointing towards the dining room door. A
                white gloved hand holds the gun.*)

MILDRED   (*off*) He certainly did . . . in his fine uniform.
                The girls used to flock around him. Now where
                did I put that book?

                (MILDRED *appears at the dining room door.
                She sees the gun and figure beyond and lets
                out an involuntary shriek.*)

                (*relaxing*) You gave me such a shock. So
                you've found . . .

                (*A shot rings out.* JOAN *jumps.* MILDRED
                *staggers back into the dining room, out of
                view. The gun barrel disappears from view.*)

JOAN   Mildred! Mildred!

                (JOAN *moves to the dining room door and then
                briefly into the dining room. There is several
                seconds silence before* DOROTHY *bursts in from
                the hall.*)

DOROTHY   (*panicking*) What is it? What's happened?

                (JOAN *appears at the dining room door.*)

JOAN   (*calmly*) It really is quite unfortunate. I seem to
                bring people such awfully bad luck. Your
                aunt's been shot dead.

                (*Blackout.*)

ACT ONE

Scene Two

The following morning. They are all assembled in the lounge. The doors to the hall and dining room are closed. JOAN *is sitting by the fire, knitting.* ELIZABETH *is sitting on the settee,* MARGARET *is sitting down right.* DOROTHY *and* CHARLES *are standing in front of the sideboard,* DOROTHY *looking distraught.* PIERRE *stands at the window, gazing outside.* BUNTING *is standing in front of the hall door.* CONSTABLE THOMKINS *is also present. He is a typical young village policeman. He stands, hands behind his back.*

MARGARET   (*irritated*) Just exactly how long do you intend to keep us all waiting here, Constable? Thirty minutes and absolutely nothing has happened.

THOMKINS   I'm sure it won't be long, Madam. The Inspector's just familiarising himself with the layout of the house.

JOAN   Tell me, Constable Thomkins, I was wondering if it might be one of the Inspectors with whom I've worked on a previous occasion?

THOMKINS   I don't believe so, Miss Maple. Actually he's an acting Inspector. Apparently there's a very nasty flu virus over at Milton . . . plain clothes are a bit thin on the ground.

MARGARET   So in fact we're being kept waiting by a Sergeant! I don't see the necessity . . . we gave you our statements last night.

CHARLES   Calm down, old girl. Get nowhere by trying to rush things. Expect they're just following routine. Got to have routine in the services. Lose your discipline if you don't.

DOROTHY   (*sobbing*) I don't care how long they keep us here . . . as long as they find out who killed poor Aunt Mildred. How could anybody . . .

(*She breaks down in tears.* CHARLES *puts an arm around* DOROTHY'S *shoulder and guides her to sit on the settee.*)

CHARLES   Sit yourself down, m'dear. Dashed rotten business but we've got to keep the old stiff upper lip, eh?

DOROTHY   But she was just lying there . . . with blood everywhere.

THOMKINS   (*to* BUNTING) Perhaps you might give the young lady a drink, Mister Bunting.

BUNTING   Very well, sir, as you like.

(BUNTING *moves to the sideboard, pours a drink for* DOROTHY *and takes a quick drink from the bottle when no one is looking. He passes the glass to* DOROTHY.)

Here you are, Miss Dorothy.

DOROTHY   Thank you.

(DOROTHY *takes a sip as* BUNTING *returns to his position at the door.*)

CHARLES   That's the ticket, m'dear. That'll soon calm you down.

DOROTHY   Yes.

CHARLES   Try not to think about it. Best way.

DOROTHY   (*attempting to smile*) Yes I know. I'll be all right in a moment.

(DOROTHY *quietly tries to compose herself. There is a brief silence.*)

JOAN   (*thinking out loud*) A bullet does such terrible damage to the skull at close range.

(DOROTHY *immediately breaks down again.*)

CHARLES   Really, Miss Maple . . . do you have to!

JOAN   Oh, I'm terribly sorry . . . how thoughtless of
                 me. (*Pause.*) It's just that I've grown so used
                 to these things . . . the blood and the brains.

                 (DOROTHY *lets out a loud wail. The others look
                 at* JOAN *in disgust.* INSPECTOR PRATT *enters
                 suddenly from the hall. As he opens the door,*
                 BUNTING *is knocked to one side.* PRATT *is
                 wearing a long overcoat and a hat which he
                 removes upon entering the room. He is an
                 inept, posing, and clumsy walking disaster
                 area. Upon entering, he stands in silence for a
                 moment, surveying the room.*)

PRATT   Ah. So . . . this'll be the lounge.

                 (PRATT *scribbles in a note book.*)

MARGARET   Have we been kept waiting all this time just so
                 that you can make such an obvious deduction,
                 Sergeant?

PRATT   Inspector. Inspector Pratt. Yes it was obvious,
                 Missus er . . .

MARGARET   Craddock.

PRATT   . . . Missus Craddock. That's the way I work.
                 Start with the unmistakeable, then proceed to
                 the un-unmistakeable.

                 (*A look of uncertainty passes over* PRATT'S *face
                 as he tries to grapple with the correct word
                 for un-unmistakeable. Giving up, he paces the
                 room to the fireplace and suddenly pounces
                 onto the wooden elephant, examining it
                 closely.*)

Was it obvious to any of you that this elephant has recently been roasted? (*Pause, then smugly.*) No, I thought not.

CHARLES It's more usual for elephants to be poached, old boy.

(PRATT *throws* CHARLES *a piercing glance.*)

Hmn . . . just trying to lighten up the proceedings.

PRATT And you are?

CHARLES Charles Craddock . . . Colonel Charles Craddock . . . retired.

PRATT I see. The wife of Missus Craddock here.

(PRATT *replaces the elephant and leans casually with his hand on the wall over the mantelpiece.*)

Is everyone assembled, Thompson?

THOMKINS Thomkins, sir.

PRATT (*looking* THOMKINS *up and down disapprovingly*) Hmn . . . quite.

THOMKINS They're all here, sir.

PRATT Good. Then I'll begin.

(THOMKINS *takes a notebook out of his tunic pocket. As* PRATT *moves from the fireplace, he notices that he has left dirty charcoal marks on the wall. He turns back to the wall, tries unsuccessfully to wipe the marks off, then moves quickly away.*)

I should listen very closely to this, Thompson. You might learn something. We're a bit more sophisticated down in Milton than out here in the sticks.

THOMKINS   Sophisticated . . . yes, sir. (*Having already judged* PRATT'S *measure.*) Is that one F or two, sir?

(PRATT *scowls at* THOMKINS.)

PRATT   I've assembled you all here to ask you a few questions about the unfortunate and regrettable circumstantials of yesterday.

ELIZABETH   Excuse me, Inspector, but we gave statements to one of the gentlemen last night.

PRATT   I'm quite aware of that, but I wanted to see you all myself. A good detective can spot a villain a mile off at close range. (*Hurriedly, realising his mistake.*) You are?

ELIZABETH   (*with her most seductive voice and smile*) Elizabeth . . . Elizabeth Hartley-Trumpington.

(PRATT *is mesmerised and stares at* ELIZABETH *for several seconds, smiling and nodding. He suddenly comes to his senses and moves away, loosening his tie slightly.*)

PRATT   Mmn. So, we are all in the very room where Missus Bagshot was so cruelly and brutally cut down last night. What I would like . . .

THOMKINS   Excuse me, sir.

PRATT   Yes, Thompson?

THOMKINS   Thomkins, sir.

PRATT   Yes, what is it?

THOMKINS   Missus Bagshot wasn't actually in this room at the time, sir. (*Pointing.*) She was in the dining room . . . by the door, sir.

PRATT	I was quite aware of that fact.
THOMKINS	Sorry, sir.
PRATT	As I was saying, the shot which so fatally killed Missus Bagshot was fired from this very room. What I would like . . .
THOMKINS	Sorry again, sir.
PRATT	(*irritated*) Now what is it!
THOMKINS	The shot wasn't fired from in here, sir. The murderer was in the hall and fired through the doorway . . . sir.
PRATT	(*even more irritated*) Thank you very much. I really don't think we need to be such sticklebacks for detail, Thompson.
THOMKINS	Thomkins, sir.
PRATT	(*collecting his thoughts, with barely controlled anger*) The bullet, which killed Missus Bagshot, passed through this very room in which we are now assembled . . .

(PRATT *looks pointedly at* THOMKINS.)

THOMKINS	Without doubt, sir.
PRATT	First of all, I'd like you all to take up the positions in which you were in when the fateful occurrence occurred.

(PRATT *stands back with a satisfied expression. The others look at him in disbelief, then, with the exception of* JOAN, *begin to file out of the room.* PRATT *watches in surprise.*)

PRATT	Where are you going?

(*They all stop.*)

MARGARET   To do as you asked, Sergeant.

THOMKINS   (*helpfully*) They were all elsewhere except for
            one, sir.

            (PRATT *takes* THOMKINS *to one side.*)

PRATT   Then why did you assemble them in here?

THOMKINS   (*bewildered*) You asked me to, sir. In the
            lounge you said, sir.

PRATT   Are you trying to make me look a fool,
            Thompson!

THOMKINS   No, sir. That's the last thing you need.

PRATT   (*poking* THOMKINS *with his finger*) You'll need
            to buck your ideas up if you want to make
            anything of yourself in the force. (*To the
            others.*) For the sake of briefness of brevity I'll
            conduct the questioning in here.

            (*They all return to their original places,
            grumbling quietly.*)

BUNTING   I wish he'd make his mind up.

            (*As they settle*, PRATT *turns to them, his back to*
            JOAN.)

PRATT   So . . . which one of you was in here when
            young Missus Bagshot was so cruelly cut
            down in her prime?

JOAN   I fear it was me, Inspector.

            (PRATT *jumps in surprise at the voice behind
            him, then spins around to face* JOAN.)

PRATT   And you are?

JOAN   Miss Maple.

PRATT	I see. And your surname, Miss Mabel?
THOMKINS	Maple is her surname, sir. She's somewhat of a celebrity in the village.
PRATT	Right. Thank you, Thompson.
JOAN	Thomkins, Inspector.
PRATT	Quite. And the reason for your celibacy, Miss Mabel?
JOAN	It's hardly that, Inspector. It's simply that I've been involved with this kind of thing many times.
PRATT	Murder!
JOAN	Most regrettably, yes, Inspector.
PRATT	I see. Regrettable indeed. So . . . you were the only person alone in the room . . . (*Glancing at* THOMKINS.) . . . when the bullet passed through. Did you see anything?
JOAN	I'm afraid not, Inspector. It was travelling rather too fast.
PRATT	(*wisely*) Yes . . . as I suspected. (*He mimes the swift passage of a bullet with a sweep of his hand.*)
JOAN	I remember her last words . . . she must have caught sight of the murderer. She said . . . "so you've found" . . . then the shot was fired. I ran to her, but upon examination she was dead.
PRATT	I see. Did she say anything?
JOAN	No, Inspector.
PRATT	Thank you, Miss Marble.

JOAN

It's my pleasure, Inspector. I only wish I could be of more help. However, I hope you won't mind me saying that it would perhaps be less confusing if you simply called me Joan.

PRATT

(*looking at* JOAN *dubiously*) Mmn. (*Suddenly spinning around.*) Colonel Craddock?

CHARLES

Yes, old boy?

PRATT

It was your gun that was used to perpetuate the crime to happen.

CHARLES

'Fraid so. Some bounder stole it from the hall.

PRATT

Careless . . . very careless indeed.

(PRATT *leans casually against the dining room door, which opens. He staggers out of sight into the dining room. He reappears several seconds later.*)

(*trying to be matter of fact*) Just checking on the dining room.

(PRATT *pauses for thought, but obviously has none whatsoever.*)

So . . . if we piece all that together, what have we got? . . . (*Picking on* THOMKINS *like a schoolmaster with a pupil.*) Thompson?

THOMKINS

I don't know, sir. Missus Bagshot may have been trying to say, "so you've found your gun", implying that she saw the Colonel.

PRATT

Exactly. I was wondering how long that would take you, Thompson. What do you say to that, Colonel?

CHARLES

Preposterous! I was in the lavatory down the hall.

PRATT

Do you have witnesses?

CHARLES	Of course I don't, man. Chap doesn't take witnesses to the little boy's room. Not unless he's up to no good of course.
PRATT	According to the statements, your wife was in her room. What about you, Miss Hartley . . . er . . .
ELIZABETH	(*smiling sweetly*) Trumpington. I was changing. Pierre had just carried up my bags for me.
PRATT	Changing . . . (*Day dreaming.*) So you were scantily clad . . . in your underwear.
ELIZABETH	(*seductive*) Quite naked, Inspector.
PRATT	Mmn . . .

(*He stares at* ELIZABETH *a little too long before breaking away.*)

Pierre . . . our mysterious Frenchman. (*Turning to* PIERRE, *and with an appalling accent.*) Bonjour mon amigo.

PIERRE	Bonjour Inspecteur. Je vous aiderai de mon mieux.

(PRATT *nods knowingly at* PIERRE, *obviously not having understood a single word.*)

PRATT	Where wassey vous when le shirt was fire-ed?
PIERRE	Pardon?
ELIZABETH	Pierre does speak excellent English, Inspector.
PRATT	Ah. Well in that case I'll conduct my inquiring questions in English . . . for those not as affluent as I. (*To* PIERRE, *very slowly and loudly.*) Where . . . were . . . you . . . when . . .

the shot . . . (*Miming a gun being fired.*) . . . bang . . . was fired?

PIERRE   (*equally slowly*) I . . . also . . . was in . . . (*Miming going through a door.*) . . . my room.

PRATT   (*miming, poiting to his eye and then making a wave motion with his hand*) I see. That leaves two unaccounted for.

(PRATT *notices* DOROTHY *and moves behind the settee. He leans over the back of the settee, between* DOROTHY *and* ELIZABETH.)

(*loudly*) Your name?

(DOROTHY'S *nerves are still on edge and she jumps, startled.*)

DOROTHY   Dorothy Foxton. Mildred was my Aunty.

PRATT   Mmm. That would make you her nephew.

DOROTHY   Her niece, Inspector. I helped her.

PRATT   I see. She had trouble getting about?

DOROTHY   Not really, no.

PRATT   So why mention her knees?

DOROTHY   I didn't! Look, I live here. I was in the kitchen when I heard the shot.

THOMKINS   There is a connecting door from the dining room to the kitchen, sir.

PRATT   I had noticed that, Thompson.

THOMKINS   Sorry, sir.

PRATT   (*to* DOROTHY) So, what did you do?

(PRATT *glances over at* ELIZABETH *and becomes mesmerised. He stares at her admiringly, barely paying any attention to* DOROTHY.)

DOROTHY   I ran into the hall . . . there was nobody there, so I came in here and found . . . (*Beginning to sob again.*) Aunty.

(*There is a pause.* PRATT *suddenly realises that* DOROTHY *has stopped speaking and stands suddenly, turning to* BUNTING.)

PRATT   (*absently*) Thank you, Miss Foxglove. (*To* BUNTING.) So, that just leaves you.

BUNTING   Bunting, sir.

PRATT   Yes, I'd deducted that. The faithful family container. Where were you?

BUNTING   The cellar, sir . . . stock-taking.

PRATT   And where is the cellar?

BUNTING   (*pointing downwards*) Down there, sir.

PRATT   (*impatient*) Where is the door?

BUNTING   At the end of the hall, sir.

PRATT   I see. You can show me it later.

BUNTING   As you like, sir . . . it's just an ordinary door, sir.

(PRATT *pauses for thought.*)

PRATT   Very interesting . . . very interesting indeed. So where does that leave us, Thompson?

THOMKINS   Seven possible suspects and not a corroborated alibi between them, sir.

CHARLES	Look here, Inspector, you can't think it was one of us. Respectable people, dash it!
PRATT	And you have a better theory?
CHARLES	Course I have. Thought you'd work it out yourself. Burglar feller enters house . . . finds gun . . . spotted by Mildred . . . Blighter shoots her.
PRATT	That is a possibility, Colonel. Quite a strong possibility.
THOMKINS	But Missus Bagshot does seem to have recognised her killer, sir.
PRATT	(*hurriedly*) Which is why I immediately dismissed it. Why are you trying to cast suspicion elsewhere, Colonel? Keep an eye on him, Thompson.
CHARLES	What are you suggesting! Complete balderdash!
PRATT	So . . . where do we go from here?
JOAN	I suspect I know where you're leading, Inspector.
PRATT	(*surprised*) You do? Well perhaps these good people don't share our little secret, Missus Marbles.
JOAN	In my experience, it's a most crucial point.
PRATT	(*knowingly*) Oh yes . . . the utmost cruciallity. (*He pauses for a further prompt, but receives none.*) I'll let you take over, Thompson . . . it'll be good experience for you.
THOMKINS	Thank you, sir. I assume we're looking for a motive, sir?
JOAN	Well done, Constable.

PRATT	Exactly. What was the motive?
THOMKINS	I don't know, sir.
JOAN	There may be a will, Constable. Invariably a very good starting point.
THOMKINS	Thank you. Does anybody know . . .
PRATT	Thank you, Thompson . . . I'll take over now. Does anyone know of a will?
DOROTHY	I think I may be able to help you, Inspector. Aunty mentioned it to me once . . . I believe it's held by the solicitor.
PRATT	And do you know the terms?
DOROTHY	No . . . no, I'm afraid not.
PRATT	Pity. Anybody else?
BUNTING	Begging your pardon, your worship.
PRATT	(*turning to* BUNTING) Inspector will suffice.
MARGARET	(*quietly*) Or Sergeant.
BUNTING	Missus Bagshot did once say that if anything happened to her she'd leave me a small pension. Will that be all right, sir?
PRATT	I'm afraid that's not up to me. Do you know anything else?
BUNTING	Well I did once accidentally hear her telling someone else about the will, but I didn't catch the details.
PRATT	And who was she talking to?
BUNTING	I can't say, sir. I don't want to get anyone into trouble.

CHARLES

(*suddenly*) Trouble! That's it . . . that's how I know your face . . . some kind of trouble. Have you ever been to India, Bunting?

PRATT

(*indignant*) If you don't mind, Colonel, I'm asking the questions. (*Composing himself.*) Have you ever been to India, Mister Bumsting?

BUNTING

No, sir.

PRATT

(*sadly*) Pity. Another dead end.

(PRATT *is silent, forgetting his line of inquiry.*)

THOMKINS

I think Mister Bunting was going to tell us about the will, sir.

PRATT

I know, Thompson, I hadn't forgotten. (*Turning to* BUNTING.) Will . . . well?

BUNTING

I don't remember, sir.

PRATT

Don't remember what?

BUNTING

The question, sir. It's the shock, sir . . . my legs have turned to jelly.

PRATT

Come, Mister Bumsting . . . don't trifle with me. You were going to tell us . . . Thompson?

THOMKINS

Who knew about the will.

PRATT

Well done . . . just checking. (*To* BUNTING.) So?

BUNTING

(*reluctantly*) It was Miss Dorothy, sir.

(*There are gasps from* ELIZABETH, MARGARET *and* CHARLES.)

PRATT

Ah . . . now we're getting somewhere.

(*Turning importantly to* MARGARET.)

Why didn't you mention this before?

MARGARET   (*pleasantly*) Because my name isn't Dorothy.

(MARGARET *points to* DOROTHY. PRATT *nods wisely*.)

PRATT   I realise that, Missus Haddock . . . don't underestimate me.

(PRATT *turns to* DOROTHY.)

I haven't mentioned the will to you earlier, Miss Foxglove, because I felt you were already too upset. However . . .

THOMKINS   You did actually, sir.

PRATT   When?

THOMKINS   A minute ago, sir. She denied all knowledge.

PRATT   Very good, Thompson . . . you're getting the hang of it now. Why did you lie, Miss?

DOROTHY   I'm sorry, I didn't mean to. I was frightened. Aunty told me that I was to get the largest part of the estate . . . I just thought you'd suspect me.

ELIZABETH   It hardly surprises me. I had suspicions from the start, Inspector.

DOROTHY   I didn't do it. I didn't kill her. You've got to believe me.

JOAN   I believe you, my dear.

PRATT   Fortunately, Missus Marbles, I'm not so gullible. (*Dramatically.*) Miss Foxglove had a strong motive and, what's more, a very good reason. She was in the kitchen, which made it easy for her to stealthily steal into the hall where she stole the gun. Shortly after stealing the gun, she stole slyly to the doorway and shot the shot that got Miss Shogbot . . . Bogshot.

DOROTHY   (*breaking down*) I didn't!

PRATT   I think that ties things up nicely. Thompson, charge her.

THOMKINS   Pardon, sir?

PRATT   Charge her. Then we'll take her down to the station.

THOMKINS   I wonder if I might have a word, sir.

PRATT   What is it now?

(THOMKINS *is rather agitated, so* PRATT *moves to him.*)

Yes?

THOMKINS   I don't think we can charge her, sir. We don't have any real evidence.

PRATT   What's the matter with you, man . . . we can soon make some up!

THOMKINS   But if it doesn't stick, sir?

PRATT   Course it will. When I've finished with her she'll be like putty in my hands.

(PRATT *moves away.*)

THOMKINS   I was only thinking of your reputation, sir.

PRATT   What?

(PRATT *moves back to* THOMKINS.)

THOMKINS   If we couldn't make a real case.

(PRATT *thinks deeply for several seconds. He turns back to the others.*)

PRATT   Mmn. That will be all for now. Don't leave the house. I may have further interrogations and questions later.

DOROTHY   What about me?

PRATT   Same applies to you, Miss Foxglove . . . especially to you.

(*They all start to leave with the exception of* PRATT, THOMKINS *and* CHARLES.)

MARGARET   This is ridiculous. Don't leave the house indeed. I shall be reporting you, Sergeant.

JOAN   Would anyone care for a pot of tea? I do so find that it helps to calm the nerves.

(*They exit, leaving* PRATT, THOMKINS *and* CHARLES.)

CHARLES   Wondered if I could have a word, old boy? Somewhat confidential . . . delicate matter and all that.

PRATT   Yes?

CHARLES   Bit tricky. Wouldn't want my wife to get wind.

PRATT   I see. She has a history?

CHARLES   What of?

PRATT   Wind.

CHARLES   No, old boy. You've missed the point. Can I rely on your discretion?

PRATT   Naturally, Colonel. Anything you say will go no further than my ears.

CHARLES	(*uncomfortable*) I do know a bit about the will. Mildred said that she was leaving me five thousand pounds.
PRATT	I don't think that amount need concern us.
CHARLES	Bit more to it, old boy. If I happen to survive Dorothy, her share of the estate is to pass to me. Bit unlikely but . . .
THOMKINS	That would be a great deal, sir. Why leave it to you?
CHARLES	Well, that's the delicate part. Hmn . . . we were close friends.
THOMKINS	But she must have had many friends.
	(PRATT *is becoming agitated that* THOMKINS *is taking over.*)
CHARLES	Some, yes. Thing is . . . over the years . . . we had a very close friendship. Hmn . . . a liaison.
THOMKINS	An affair, sir!
CHARLES	Well I wouldn't go that far . . . more of a . . . it was a . . . hmn . . . yes.
THOMKINS	And how long has this . . .
PRATT	Do you mind, Thompson!
CHARLES	Close on thirty years. Died down a bit over recent years of course. Hate the wife to find out. Wouldn't want to upset the old apple cart, if you take my meaning.
PRATT	I see no reason why she should. We're all men of the world, Colonel.
CHARLES	Dashed grateful. All of this sets a chap's head spinning. Think that's everything though . . .

made a clean breast. Any objection if I take a turn around the garden?

PRATT
There's no need to for us to take turns, Colonel . . . I have pressing matters here.

CHARLES
(*puzzled by* PRATT's *response*) Good show. Glad we understand each other.

(CHARLES *goes to the hall door. As he opens it,* JOAN *falls in from the hall.*)

Miss Maple!

THOMKINS
We'll deal with this, sir.

CHARLES
Never seen such a thing! Can't a chap have privacy.

(CHARLES *exits, leaving* JOAN *looking sheepish.* THOMKINS *moves to her.*)

THOMKINS
I hope you weren't doing what I thought, Miss Maple.

(PRATT *is bored and moves to the desk. He picks up an ornament to examine it.*)

JOAN
Why, certainly not, Constable. I was just returning to retrieve my knitting. I seem to have mislaid it. (*She sees the knitting on the armchair.*) Ah . . . there.

(JOAN *retrieves her knitting and moves back to the hall door.*)

Would either of you care for a teacake?

THOMKINS
I wouldn't say no, Miss Maple. Very kind of you.

JOAN
And I expect the Inspector would like one as well. I won't be a moment.

(JOAN *exits.* PRATT *moves to replace the ornament but suddenly finds it to be in several pieces. He is surprised by* THOMKINS *approaching him and thrusts the pieces into his pocket.*)

THOMKINS   What do you think so far, sir?

PRATT   I don't know. It's a tricky one, Thompson.

THOMKINS   Thomkins, sir.

PRATT   So many suspects . . . not a corrugated alibi (*he pronounces it as aleebi*) between them. The woman who just left . . . the so called Mabel Marbles . . . she worries me. Why is she so keen to be known as Missus Jones?

THOMKINS   Actually, her name's Miss Maple, sir.

PRATT   Really! Or is that just another alias? By her own confession she's murdered before.

THOMKINS   No, sir . . . I think she just solves them.

PRATT   (*not listening*) And Colonel Haddock. Very fishy. Does he know more than he's saying?

THOMKINS   I doubt it, sir. Anyway, if he was guilty, why tell us so much in the first place?

PRATT   Easy. As soon as he saw me he realised he'd have to come clean. He's used to dealing with trained men. He recognised my ruthless relentless streak and knew that I'd leave no stone unturned in the pursuit of justice.

THOMKINS   (*trying to keep a straight face*) I see, sir.

PRATT   Strange that he should mention this Mildred woman. We'll need to check . . . see where she fits in to all this.

THOMKINS   She's dead, sir . . . she was murdered.

PRATT	Another one! My God, Thompson, it makes you shudder to think how far some people will go. You know, I've got a gut feeling. Dorothy Foxtrot's our man.
THOMKINS	Woman, sir.
PRATT	What?
THOMKINS	Dorothy Foxton's our woman, sir.
PRATT	Ah . . . I wondered how long it would take before you came around to my way of thinking.
THOMKINS	That's not exactly what I meant, sir. You see, you said . . .
	(PRATT *glowers at him.*)
	It doesn't matter, sir . . . but I do think there may still be one or two stones left to turn, sir.
PRATT	Are you trying to be funny, Thompson?
THOMKINS	(*innocent*) No, sir.
PRATT	Good, it doesn't suit you.
	(JOAN *enters carrying a plate of teacakes liberally spread with jam.*)
JOAN	I have your teacakes. I do so hope you like strawberry jam . . . it's rather my favourite.
THOMKINS	Thank you Miss Maple. Very kind I'm sure.
	(THOMKINS *is about to take a piece of teacake.*)
PRATT	Not while you're on duty, Thompson!
THOMKINS	Pardon, sir?

PRATT

We've got an image to maintain, man. If you want something to do, fetch me the gun. It's in my car.

(THOMKINS *is about to exit to the hall.*)

Oh . . . and do something with this.

(PRATT *takes the broken ornament from his pocket and gives it to* THOMKINS, *who looks at it in surprise before exiting.* PRATT *notices* JOAN *watching him.*)

Important evidence . . . can't leave it lying around. When Thompson comes back, I'd like to try a little experiment.

(PRATT *casually reaches out and takes a piece of teacake.*)

See if we can jog your memory, Miss Marbles.

(PRATT *takes a large bite from the teacake, leaving jam on the end of his nose.*)

JOAN

That may be helpful. You know, I feel very uneasy. At this stage I usually have a little inkling.

PRATT

Really? Well, don't let me keep you. madam . . . down the hall on the left I believe.

JOAN

(*giving* PRATT *an exasperated sideways glance before continuing*) I must say that I'm absolutely delighted that you've eliminated me from your inquiries, Inspector.

PRATT

I wouldn't say that, Miss Marbles . . . or should I call you Missus Jones? I discount and illuminate no one.

JOAN

Well in that case you really must be more careful, Inspector. If I were a deranged killer I could just have eliminated *you*.

PRATT   (*smiling smugly*) I think not. I'm a highly
                trained fighting machine.

JOAN   But I've come across so many cases of
                poisoning . . . a most unpleasant death. I do
                find it such an underhand method.

                (PRATT *laughs casually, then glances at the
                remains of the teacake in his hand with a look
                of horror. As* JOAN *turns to sit in the chair by
                the fire, he quickly looks around for
                somewhere to dispose of the teacake. Seeing
                nowhere, he thrusts it into his coat pocket.*
                THOMKINS *enters carrying a revolver.*)

PRATT   Ah, Thompson, about time.

                (PRATT *takes the gun from* THOMKINS. THOMKINS
                looks at the jam on PRATT'S *nose suspiciously.
                Throughout the next speech* PRATT *holds the
                gun uncomfortably, occasionally wiping the
                gun and his hand on his coat, as he realises
                that his hand is sticky from the jam.*)

                I intend to try an old and trusted technique to
                see if Miss Marbles can remember or recall
                anything else about the event . . . a
                reconstitution. You be Missus Bigshot,
                Thompson . . . (*Importantly.*) I'll be the killer.

JOAN   And would you like me to be myself, Inspector?

PRATT   (*thinking*) Mmn . . . good idea.

                (THOMKINS *pulls his notebook from his pocket
                and flicks through the pages.*)

THOMKINS   I have Missus Bagshot's last words recorded,
                sir.

JOAN   I believe Mildred said she was going into the
                dining room to find a book.

PRATT   Ah . . . good . . . already the plot thickens!

JOAN   You should be in the hall, Inspector.

PRATT   (*indignant*) I know . . . I was going.

    (PRATT *moves out of sight into the hall.*)

THOMKINS   (*self-consciously trying to imitate a woman*)
    I'll go into the dining room to find a book.

    (THOMKINS *moves into the dining room, hand
    on hip, trying to imitate a woman's walk. He
    reappears at the doorway a moment later.
    PRATT pokes the barrel of the revolver through
    from the hall.*)

    (*reading from his notes*) Oh . . . you gave me
    such a shock. So you've found . . .

    (*There is a shot.* THOMKINS *howls and falls
    backwards into the dining room, out of sight.
    There is a slight pause before the others react.
    JOAN hurries to the dining room door. PRATT
    enters into the lounge with a startled
    expression on his face. He keeps looking
    alternately at the gun in his hand,* JOAN *and
    the dining room, shrugging his shoulders as if
    to deny all responsibility.*)

JOAN   (*at the dining room door*) How very careless,
    Inspector. You've shot Constable Thomkins.

    (*Blackout.*)

ACT TWO

Scene One

Two hours later. CHARLES, DOROTHY *and* PIERRE *are sitting,* CHARLES *snoring softly.* MARGARET *is agitated, pacing back and forth by the window.*

MARGARET   This is absolutely absurd. What is the point of keeping us cooped up here!

PIERRE   I expect the Inspector will 'ave more questions for us on 'is return.

MARGARET   Questions! That idiot wouldn't know a sensible question if one fell out of the sky and landed in his mouth!

PIERRE   With that I 'ave to agree.

MARGARET   Why don't you do something, Charles?

(MARGARET *glances at* CHARLES *and notices that he is asleep. She moves behind him.*)

(*hissing*) Charles!

(CHARLES *merely grunts and continues to snore.*)

(*shouting*) Charles!

(CHARLES *awakes with a start.*)

CHARLES   (*half asleep*) What! . . . Form line . . . prepare to fire. (*Waking fully.*) What's happened?

MARGARET   Nothing has happened . . . that's the whole point.

CHARLES   (*mopping his forehead*) Must have nodded off. Damned tricky moment there . . . surrounded . . . Regiment of French butlers. Very odd.

MARGARET	(*resuming her pacing*) Why don't you do something about it?
CHARLES	Nothing much I could do . . . hopeless situation. Defenceless . . .
MARGARET	To get us out of here! Two hours we've been waiting and nothing!
CHARLES	Expect somebody will turn up eventually. Due process and all that.
MARGARET	(*staring at* DOROTHY) It's not as if we don't know who did it.
DOROTHY	(*miserable*) I didn't. Why won't anybody believe me.
MARGARET	Come along, Charles, you're going to make a phone call.
CHARLES	Am I? Who to?
MARGARET	The police . . . someone in authority. They can't hold us here like this.
CHARLES	Think they probably can, actually.
MARGARET	Charles, I'm not arguing! We'll use the phone upstairs . . . in private.
	(MARGARET *moves to the hall door.* CHARLES *does not move.*)
	Charles!
CHARLES	Alright, coming, old girl.
	(CHARLES *rises.*)
MARGARET	And stop calling me old girl!
CHARLES	Oh, right . . . sorry, old girl.

(MARGARET *and* CHARLES *exit to the hall.*
PIERRE *stands, a smug expression on his face.*)

PIERRE   Well, Dorothy, it seems as though your little
           scheme 'as come unglued.

DOROTHY   What scheme?

PIERRE   To kill your Aunt and 'ave 'er money. The
           police suspect you.

DOROTHY   (*cold*) But they can't prove anything.

PIERRE   But I can give them all the evidence they need
           to 'ang you. I was passing by the top of the
           stair . . . I saw you fire the shot.

DOROTHY   That's not true!

PIERRE   It matters little. They will believe me. I will tell
           them I did not come forward earlier because I
           was fond of you . . . but, now I realise my duty.

DOROTHY   (*standing*) But why, Pierre?

PIERRE   You 'ave caused me much misery. Your
           accusation about the paintings. (*Pause.*) Of
           course, we could per'aps come to an
           arrangement.

DOROTHY   But I wasn't serious about the paintings . . . I
           wouldn't have taken all the money. Just
           enough to reimburse my Aunt. I wanted to
           frighten you . . . but I didn't want you to go to
           prison.

PIERRE   Silence, Dorothy, your motives are not
           important. You are a wealthy woman now. What
           I ask is simple. You give me twenty thousand
           pounds and ignore the matter of the paintings.
           In return, I will forget what I saw. It is as easy
           as that.

DOROTHY   Really that simple?

PIERRE   (*confident*) But of course . . . I knew you would
                  listen to reason.

DOROTHY   Fine. (*Approaching* PIERRE *to confront him.*)
                  Now it's time for you to listen to me. I was
                  wrong about you, Pierre. I should have gone
                  straight to the police instead of playing games.
                  When they get back, I'll tell them everything.

PIERRE   (*shocked*) But, Dorothy . . . I will be forced to
                  tell them what I saw.

DOROTHY   And why should they believe you . . . a cheap
                  con-man! You're pathetic.

                  (DOROTHY s*pins on her heels and exits into the
                  hall.* PIERRE *is devastated. He walks slowly to
                  look at the paintings.*)

PIERRE   (*in a very English accent*) Damn . . .

                  (PIERRE *does not notice* ELIZABETH *as she enters
                  from the hall.*)

                  Damn and blast.

ELIZABETH   That sounded very English, Pierre!

                  (PIERRE *turns, shocked. He relaxes when he
                  sees it is* ELIZABETH.)

PIERRE   (*keeping the English accent*) It was about to
                  get extremely anglo-saxon. And will you stop
                  using that ridiculous accent . . . it frightened
                  me to death.

ELIZABETH   (*in a broad Cockney accent*) It gets to be a
                  'abbit. Did it work then?

PIERRE   What do you think! She's going to tell the
                  police everything.

ELIZABETH   You bleedin' blew it!

PIERRE	I did everything you said. We're going to have to get out of here fast.
ELIZABETH	What good would that do? They'd get us before we'd got five mile. I told you before . . . there's only one way out.
PIERRE	We can't kill her!
ELIZABETH	Why not . . . interferin' bitch! You weren't bothered about Bagshot.
PIERRE	Missus Bagshot was different!
ELIZABETH	Why? You goin' soft? Do you fancy 'er or somethin'?
PIERRE	Of course not.
ELIZABETH	She's the only thing standin' in our way. If she spills the beans we're finished. We got things perfect . . . I find the rich old fools, you relieve 'em of their money . . . why spoil all that?
PIERRE	I don't know. I need to think.
ELIZABETH	We 'aven't got *time* to think!

(JOAN's *voice is heard in the hall.*)

| JOAN | (*off*) Perhaps you'd care to join us for afternoon tea later, Missus Craddock. |

(JOAN *enters from the hall. As she enters,* PIERRE *and* ELIZABETH *revert immediately to their false accents.*)

| ELIZABETH | It's just so ghastly, Pierre. How could anyone do that to such a kind old lady. Ah, Miss Maple . . . we were just talking about poor Missus Bagshot. |

JOAN

Quite tragic, my dear. Such a sad loss. I partly blame myself . . . I seem to bring such misfortune.

(JOAN *sits by the fire.*)

Do sit down. I do so love a cosy chat.

ELIZABETH

I'm terribly sorry, Miss Maple, but you will have to excuse us. We were about to take a walk in the grounds. It's so claustrophobic being kept here . . . quite ghastly.

JOAN

A walk? What a good idea. Would you mind very much if I joined you?

ELIZABETH

(*seeing no way out*) No . . . of course not, delighted.

JOAN

I'm afraid that I don't walk as briskly as I used to, but the countryside is so pleasant at this time of year. My nephew often escorts me . . . (*Rather caustically.*) . . . when he has the time.

ELIZABETH

How marvellous. Oh . . .

(ELIZABETH *suddenly holds her forehead delicately and sways slightly.*)

JOAN

Are you unwell, my dear?

(PIERRE *moves to support* ELIZABETH.)

ELIZABETH

Thank you, Pierre. Just a slight fainting fit. I have them often.

(PIERRE *helps* ELIZABETH *into a chair.*)

It will pass in a moment. Then perhaps Pierre might help me to my room.

PIERRE

It would be my pleasure.

(BUNTING *suddenly bursts into the room from the hall. He has been drinking heavily and walks unsteadily, waving a brandy bottle from which he takes occasional drinks. His speech is slurred.*)

BUNTING   (*waving*) Hello everyone. What are you doing?

JOAN   Why, Mister Bunting, I do believe you've been drinking!

BUNTING   I've had a drop. (*Staggering to* JOAN *and waving the bottle in her face.*) Do you want a swig?

JOAN   I don't believe so. Most kind. I really think that perhaps you should sit down.

BUNTING   Don't want to . . . I'm cebrelating. It's the happiest day of my life.

JOAN   Oh, I don't think you mean that, Mister Bunting.

BUNTING   Yes I do. I'm cebrelating because . . . because . . . (*Confronting* JOAN *with a puzzled expression.*) Why am I cebrelating?

JOAN   I really don't know, Mister Bunting.

BUNTING   That's funny . . . neither do I.

(BUNTING *staggers away from* JOAN, *to the centre of the room. He smiles inanely at* ELIZABETH, *who looks away in disgust. He points at her.*)

She's stuck up, she is.

(*He notices* PIERRE *and attempts to focus on him before staggering up to him.*)

Hallo, Frenchie . . . do you want a drink?

PIERRE	(*distasteful*) Non.
BUNTING	(*imitating* PIERRE) Non . . . oui . . . non.

(BUNTING *find this hilarious and staggers away, muttering to himself.*)

Oui . . . non . . . oui . . . non. (*With sudden inspiration.*) I'm rich. She's deaded and I'm rich. That's what I'm cebrelating.

(MARGARET *and* CHARLES *enter from the hall.*)

MARGARET	There he is, Charles . . . disgusting.
BUNTING	(*waving happily at* MARGARET) Hello . . . I'm rich.
MARGARET	Get him out of here, Charles, before he breaks something.
CHARLES	Do my best. Come on, old boy.

(BUNTING *staggers up to* CHARLES, *face to face, breathing heavily on him.*)

BUNTING	I don't like you.
CHARLES	(*sniffing*) Good God . . . that's Napoleon Brandy . . . recognise it anywhere.
MARGARET	Does it matter!
CHARLES	Course it matters . . . damned waste. Come on, man, can you walk?
BUNTING	Course I can walk . . . I can walk anywhere I want.

(BUNTING *tries to walk along an imaginary straight line. It's path takes him directly to the settee, which he starts to climb.* CHARLES *drags him off and towards the hall door.* MARGARET *takes* BUNTING'S *other arm and they lead him away.* BUNTING'S *legs keep collapsing beneath him.*)

CHARLES   Bad form, man. Never seen anything like it!

MARGARET   We'll take him to his room, Charles . . . out of the way.

                 (*As they exit*, JOAN *rises and moves away into the dining room.*)

JOAN   I'll make him a pot of tea. I always find it sobers me enormously.

                 (ELIZABETH *and* PIERRE *are left alone. They adopt their real accents.*)

ELIZABETH   Well . . . what do you think?

PIERRE   I don't know. I suppose you're right.

ELIZABETH   Course I'm right. We're goin' to 'ave to do it straight away. If we're clever we can frame that drunken old fool. (*Laughing.*) The state he's in we can get away with murder.

                 (DOROTHY *enters from the hall.* PIERRE *and* ELIZABETH *adopt their false accents.*)

                 Dorothy . . . how nice of you to join us.

DOROTHY   It looks as though Bunting is enjoying himself. Perhaps you should have a last drink, Pierre . . . I don't think you're going to get another one for a long time.

ELIZABETH   Are you going away, Pierre? How exciting . . . somewhere exotic?

DOROTHY   I don't think it could be described as exotic, do you, Pierre? Very cheap though.

                 (DOROTHY *moves to look at the paintings, her back to* PIERRE. *During the following conversation,* ELIZABETH *edges to the hall door to keep watch.* PIERRE *picks up a cushion from the settee and attempts to creep up behind* DOROTHY *to suffocate her.*)

There's something you ought to know about Pierre, Elizabeth. And I need a little insurance by telling someone.

ELIZABETH   Really? How intriguing.

(ELIZABETH *nods encouragingly at* PIERRE, *who edges closer to* DOROTHY.)

DOROTHY   These paintings are forgeries. He cheated my Aunt. He'll try to deny it but I have all the proof I need. I've written a full statement which is under lock and key in the safe.

(DOROTHY *turns to face* PIERRE *just in time. He drops his arms.*)

(*smiling*) I hope you weren't thinking of doing anything silly, Pierre. There's no way out now that Elizabeth knows.

ELIZABETH   But this is ghastly! Pierre, is it true?

DOROTHY   Oh, it's true all right.

(DOROTHY *turns back to the paintings.*)

(ELIZABETH *nods at* PIERRE *who approaches behind* DOROTHY *again.*)

I believe he's also sold paintings to your father, Elizabeth. It wouldn't surprise me if they were forgeries too. (PIERRE *is about to pounce.*) Your father should check.

(PIERRE *is stopped in mid stride by the sound of* CHARLES *in the hall.* ELIZABETH *shakes her head at him, telling him to stop. He throws the cushion back onto the settee.*)

CHARLES	(*off*) That's the trick, Miss Maple . . . plenty of hot drinks down him. Ah, Elizabeth . . .
	(CHARLES *enters from the hall*.)
	Got the chap down there at last. (*Crossing to the sideboard.*) Terrible thing is drink. Anyone care to join me for one?
	(*They all decline.*)
	Suit yourselves. Course, that chap's drunk all the decent stuff.
	(CHARLES *picks up a decanter and a glass and moves to sit by the fire. During the following conversation he refills his glass several times.*)
	Shouldn't really drink alone. Leads to melancholy, y'know. (*Noticing the tension.*) All damned quiet . . . anything the matter?
ELIZABETH	No, Colonel. It's just so difficult to be enthusiastic about anything . . . under the circumstances.
CHARLES	Ah, yes . . . quite. A glass of this wouldn't do you any harm. I expect you know a thing or two about drinking, Mister er . . . hmn. Land of the vineyard and all that.
PIERRE	It is true, we 'ave the finest wines in the world. But I believe that good wines should be drunk in moderation, to tantalise the palate.
CHARLES	Really? Strange attitude! Still, each to his own I suppose.
PIERRE	Now, if you will excuse me, I 'ave things to attend to.
DOROTHY	(*pleasantly*) Don't stray too far, Pierre.

PIERRE   Believe me, Dorothy, I will not.

                (PIERRE *exits to the hall, exchanging glances*
                with ELIZABETH. *He signals "two minutes,*
                upstairs" to her.)

CHARLES   Odd chap . . . something damned suspicious
                about him. Foreign . . . eyes too close together.

DOROTHY   He's not all he seems, Colonel.

CHARLES   Really? Thought not. Still, suppose none of us
                are. Take me for example. Been doing a spot of
                thinking since poor old Mildred . . . time to
                make a change. Life's too short for pretending.

DOROTHY   But you don't pretend anything, Colonel. I've
                never met anyone so honest.

CHARLES   Don't you believe it, m'dear. All a front.
                Wasted my life . . . never achieved a thing.

DOROTHY   But all your travelling . . . adventure . . . India.

CHARLES   Adventure! Joined the army because I had to
                . . . family tradition. Soon realised I wasn't up
                to it . . . damned coward, y'see. My Father
                pulled a few strings . . . made sure I spent all
                my time sitting behind a desk.

DOROTHY   But all your stories about India!

CHARLES   Only been there once . . . two weeks. I started
                making up little stories . . . make myself a bit
                more interesting. Told 'em so many times I
                ended up believing 'em myself. Couldn't stop.
                Only Margaret knew the truth . . . and old
                Mildred, of course. So you see . . . I'm not all I
                seem either. Nothing but a fake.

DOROTHY   No you're not, Colonel . . . I know a fake when I
                see one.

                (ELIZABETH *begins to look anxious.*)

CHARLES	(*staring into his glass, mournfully*) Knew this stuff would start to make me melancholy. (*More cheerful.*) Still . . . I've drunk it now. (*Raising his glass.*) Here's to Mildred . . . wherever she is.

(CHARLES *downs the remainder of his drink.*)

ELIZABETH	Dorothy, I was wondering if you'd care to come up to my room. I have a present for you, some perfume.
DOROTHY	For me?
ELIZABETH	I know we haven't always hit it off, but I'd so like us to be friends. Would you like to come up?
DOROTHY	(*hesitant, looking at* CHARLES) I don't know . . . I . . .
CHARLES	You two get off. Don't want to hang about listening to an old duffer like me. Go on . . . enjoy yourselves.
DOROTHY	(*smiling*) All right. But you're not an old duffer.

(DOROTHY *moves to* CHARLES *and kisses him lightly on the forehead.*)

You meant a lot to my aunt.

(DOROTHY *and* ELIZABETH *move to exit to the hall. They stop as* PRATT *enters.* ELIZABETH *becomes increasingly agitated as the remainder of the scene progresses.*)

PRATT	Come on, Thompson, it's only a scratch.

(THOMKINS *hobbles in behind* PRATT. *His foot is heavily bandaged and he walks with the aid of a stick. He has a pained expression.*)

Afternoon, all.

THOMKINS   Is it all right if I sit down for a moment, sir? I'm feeling rather faint.

PRATT   Faint! Don't know what's wrong with you, man. Superficial flesh wound . . . I've had worse from a flea bite. (*Relenting.*) Two minutes, then you're back on the job.

            (THOMKINS *sits, thankfully.*)

CHARLES   Don't know why you've brought the chap back here! Ought to be resting. Don't want gangrene to set in.

THOMKINS   (*looking queasy*) I'm all right, sir. The Inspector thought I ought to keep moving.

CHARLES   Pity you weren't moving a bit faster a couple of hours ago, he might have missed you!

PRATT   (*proudly*) I've had full weapons training, Colonel . . . I never miss.

CHARLES   Damn it all . . . sounds as if you meant to shoot the poor blighter. Foolhardy if you ask me.

PRATT   But I don't ask you, Colonel. And might I remind you that you are still under suspicion of being a suspect. Tread warily, sir.

CHARLES   (*pointing to* THOMKINS) Like him!

ELIZABETH   Come along, Dorothy . . . we'll be upstairs, Inspector.

PRATT   Very good, Miss.

DOROTHY   Just a moment. I need to speak to you, Inspector.

            (*The telephone rings.* DOROTHY *answers it.*)

Hallo, Bagshot House . . . yes, yes he is. I'll get him for you. It's for you, Inspector.

PRATT   (*importantly*) Ah . . . that'll be for me. Who is it?

DOROTHY   The Deputy Chief Constable.

PRATT   (*nervous*) Ah . . . are you sure he wanted me? Did he mention my name . . . it might be for Thompson.

DOROTHY   I think his exact words were, "Is the idiot whose in charge of the investigation there?"

THOMKINS   (*cheerfully*) Oh, it is for you, sir.

             (PRATT *scowls at* THOMKINS *and reluctantly takes the phone from* DOROTHY.)

PRATT   Pratt . . . no, not you, sir. I'm Pratt . . . yes, very apt, sir . . . well, it's just a scratch really . . . same weapon, yes, sir . . . complaint? But I'm very close to an arrest . . . very good, sir . . . (*It seems that the receiver has been slammed down at the other end.*) . . . sir? . . . hallo? . . . (*With feeling.*) Perhaps if you got your fat bottom out of that chair once in a while. (*Startled, suddenly realising that he hasn't been cut off.*) . . . Sorry, sir! Thought you'd gone, sir.

             (PRATT *winces as the phone obviously is slammed down at the other end. He sadly replaces the receiver.*)

THOMKINS   He sounded on good form, sir.

PRATT   Good form? Yes. He's very pleased with progress. Unfortunately it would seem that someone rang him . . . made allegations. On your foot, Thompson, I want to get it wrapped up once and for all.

(THOMKINS *reluctantly struggles to his feet.*)

It appears that we're not . . . you're not doing your job properly, Thompson. Incompetent. It wouldn't be you would it, Colonel? Are you the alligator?

CHARLES   As a matter of fact, old boy, I did make the odd call.

PRATT   Aha . . . watch him very closely, Thompson . . . trouble maker.

CHARLES   No need to take it personally, y'know. Wasn't casting aspersions. I simply said that things seemed to be dragging a bit this end and could they speed things up yours.

PRATT   (*indignant*) Speed things up! I'll speed things up so much you'll wish . . . you'll wish . . . well you'll jolly well wish they weren't. What do you say to that, Colonel Haddock?

(MARGARET *enters from the hall.*)

MARGARET   Oh no . . . it's you again, Sergeant.

PRATT   Inspector!

CHARLES   Really! Got the impression from the call that you were probably down to Constable by now!

PRATT   Thompson, if the Colonel opens his mouth again, book it.

THOMKINS   Yes, sir. (*Thinking.*) What for, sir?

PRATT   Anything! Use your imagination, man. Disturbing the police . . . loitering with a tent.

MARGARET   May I ask when we will be allowed to leave, Sergeant? I see nothing to be gained by our presence and I'd rather like to get away before you shoot someone else.

PRATT   (*barely controlling his temper*) Missus Haddock, please don't push me further. You can learn from this, Thompson. You'll come across all kinds of provocation, but you must always keep a cool, clear, empty head. Otherwise you'll cease to function as a finely tuned crime detection machine. (*Proudly.*) I've learnt this from my twenty years on the force.

CHARLES   And how many Constables have you shot in that time?

PRATT   (*in a rage*) Book him, Thompson . . . book him!

DOROTHY   May I have a word now, Inspector?

PRATT   No you may not! I'm in charge.

(JOAN *enters from the hall.*)

JOAN   Good afternoon, Inspector, how pleasant. Oh, and Constable Thomkins. I do hope your foot isn't causing too much distress.

THOMKINS   Not too bad, thank you, Miss Maple. Rather throbbing though.

(PRATT *is impatient.*)

JOAN   I expect so. Bullet wounds can be very troublesome. I always recommend a poultice of cold herbal tea for any open wound.

THOMKINS   Really? My Aunty Doris swears by boiled cabbage.

PRATT   Thompson, do you mind!

THOMKINS   Sorry, sir.

PRATT   I'd like to continue by . . .

JOAN   I'd be very interested in details of the cabbage
                preparation, Constable. Perhaps you might give
                it to me later.

PRATT   I'd like to continue by . . .

JOAN   Mind you, the price of vegetables can be quite
                prohibitive at this time of year. Fortunately I
                have a small vegetable plot.

PRATT   Missus Marbles.

JOAN   Yes, Inspector?

PRATT   May I be allowed to carry on?

JOAN   But of course, Inspector. I'm so interested to
                hear your next line of inquiry.

PRATT   Thank you. I'd like to continue by . . .

JOAN   Just one moment, before you recommence,
                Inspector, but a certain matter had completely
                slipped my mind. I wonder if I might enquire
                whether you and the Constable might be
                joining us for afternoon tea? I phoned Mister
                Coupling in the village and asked him to deliver
                here. He really does make exceedingly fine
                cream fancies.

PRATT   (incredulous) Is that all!

JOAN   Oh dear. I fear I've upset you, Inspector.
                Perhaps you would have preferred an
                individual fruit tart?

PRATT   I live in hope that we will be finished here long
                before tea. Now I'd like to continue by
                conducting another small experiment. Fetch the
                gun, Thompson.

MARGARET   You're not fetching that thing in here with me!

PRATT	Rest assured, Madam, there'll be no more incendiary incidents . . . I think Thompson's learnt his lesson.
THOMKINS	Where is the gun, sir?
PRATT	I don't know. I gave it to you!
THOMKINS	I don't think so, sir. I was holding my foot if you remember, sir.
JOAN	I can confirm that, Inspector. I have a very good memory for detail.
PRATT	Then I must have left it in the dining room.
THOMKINS	Very good, sir.
	(THOMKINS *hobbles out into the dining room.*)
PRATT	It occurs to me that the bullet which perpetrated Miss Bogshot clean between the eyes was either an expert one or a lucky one.
CHARLES	Hardly lucky for her, old boy!
PRATT	Have any of you handled a gun before?
	(*They remain silent with the exception of* CHARLES.)
CHARLES	I have obviously.
PRATT	Obviously! And why should that be so obvious, Colonel?
CHARLES	Well . . . I was in the army of course!
PRATT	Really! Why have you kept this such a closely guarded secret? What rank did you attain?
CHARLES	Dash it all, man . . . it's general knowledge!
PRATT	Ah, so . . . you were a General, Colonel!

CHARLES   Don't talk balderdash, man . . . I was a Colonel!

PRATT   So why try to deceive me! Why are you so
            anxious to confuse me with red haddocks,
            Colonel Herring!

            (THOMKINS *enters from the dining room.*)

THOMKINS   It's not there, sir.

PRATT   What! It must be!

CHARLES   Damned careless if you ask me. Wasn't still
            loaded was it?

PRATT   Loaded? (*Obviously uncertain.*) Of course not,
            Colonel . . . do you take me for a fool?

JOAN   I have a sense of foreboding. I suspect that we
            may all be in terrible danger, Inspector. There's
            no telling the actions of an unhinged mind.

PRATT   (*nervous*) Nonsense. No danger at all . . .
            perfectly safe. Still, I think I've got as far as I
            can here. I'll leave you to it, Thompson. I must
            get back to the station . . . damned paperwork.

            (PRATT *moves cautiously to the hall door.*)

THOMKINS   Could I have a word, sir?

PRATT   What now, Thompson, I'm a busy man!

THOMKINS   It is important. In private if we may, sir.

            (PRATT *reluctantly decides to speak to*
            THOMKINS, *but is undecided on the safest place.*
            He peers out into the hall, then decides that
            the lounge is safer.)

PRATT   All wait out in the hall, if you please.

(All exit to the hall with the exception of PRATT *and* THOMKINS. *As they pass* PRATT, *he eyes them nervously, edging away from them. When they have exited,* PRATT *closes the door quickly and leans against it to hold it shut.)*

Get on with it then.

THOMKINS   I think the killer may have played into our hands, sir.

PRATT   Quite, Thompson. A mad man on the rampage with a gun. We've got him exactly where he wants us!

THOMKINS   I think we should send them all to their rooms, sir. Then you announce that you're going to search their rooms.

PRATT   Oh, very good, Thompson! So I walk into the lions burrow and find the killer with a gun at my head.

THOMKINS   No, I don't think so, sir. My guess is that whoever has the gun will panic and dispose of it out of the window. Their rooms all face the front of the house. I was thinking of taking a hobble onto the drive, sir.

PRATT   What for?

THOMKINS   To see where the gun comes from.

PRATT   Mmn . . . has it's merits I suppose. You search the rooms, I'll keep a look out . . . wouldn't want you getting your foot cold.

*(*PRATT *edges away from the door.)*

Off you go then, Thomkins.

THOMKINS   Thompson, sir.

(*They both suddenly realise the mistake and do a double take of each other.* THOMKINS *exits to the hall.* PRATT *nervously closes the door.*)

(*off*) Would you all retire to your rooms, please. Straight away . . . thank you.

PRATT   This had better work, man.

(PRATT *moves from the door and does not notice* DOROTHY *entering quietly behind him. She carries a handbag.*)

DOROTHY   Inspector.

(PRATT *jumps in fright and screams.*)

PRATT   Aagh!

(*He turns to see* DOROTHY *and shortens the scream into an exclamation.*)

Ah . . . Miss Foxhunt.

DOROTHY   At last I've got you alone, Inspector.

PRATT   (*nervous again*) Yes.

DOROTHY   (*cold*) I've got a confession to make . . . a score to settle. It's time for retribution.

PRATT   (*terrified*) There's really no need. We can do a deal.

DOROTHY   (*puzzled*) What sort of deal?

PRATT   Anything you like. You can just walk out of here. I won't say a word . . . I'll forget I've ever seen you. Borrow my car if you like.

DOROTHY   No, Inspector, I must finish it now.

(DOROTHY *reaches to open her handbag.* PRATT *squeals and drops to his knees.*)

PRATT   Please Missus Foxhunt . . . don't do it. I'm just
           a poor copper trying to get through to
           retirement. I wouldn't hurt a fly. Think of my
           family . . . the two little Pratts. I won't tell
           anyone you're the murderer.

           (DOROTHY *pulls a handkerchief from her
           handbag and dabs her eyes.*)

DOROTHY   But I'm not the murderer. I have some other
           information for you. Excuse me, this is all so
           upsetting.

           (DOROTHY *blows her nose.*)

PRATT   Not the murderer?

DOROTHY   No, Inspector.

           (PRATT *thinks rapidly for a moment, then starts
           to examine the carpet closely.*)

PRATT   (*matter of fact*) Quite so. I was concerned
           about this rather nasty stain on your carpet. I
           think you'll find a little warm water should do
           the trick. (*Standing.*) Now, about this other
           matter. Does your information concern the
           identity of the brutal killer and murderer?

DOROTHY   Not exactly but . . .

PRATT   Then it can wait. I have little time. Even as I
           speak I am currently implementating a daring
           plan to flush out the miscreant.

DOROTHY   But . . .

PRATT   I'm sure your information can wait five
           minutes.

DOROTHY   But . . . yes, I suppose so. (*Turning to leave,
           then back to* PRATT.) Five minutes. I'm sorry if I
           frightened you earlier.

PRATT   Frightened? Oh, don't be deceived, Miss
                   Foxhole. Just a cunning ploy to draw you into
                   making a run for it. I think I can illuminate you
                   from further inquiries.

                   (DOROTHY *exits into the hall.* PRATT *sighs with
                   relief, wipes his brow and moves to follow
                   her.*)

                   Coming Thompson, ready or not.

                   (*Two shots are heard from the hall, followed
                   by a scream from* DOROTHY. PRATT *reacts
                   instantly, screaming and hurling himself over
                   the back of the settee where he then tries to
                   burrow under the cushions.* DOROTHY *staggers
                   into view at the hall door.*)

DOROTHY   (*gasping*) He's trying to kill . . .

                   (*There is a final shot.* DOROTHY *slumps to the
                   floor. There is total silence. After several
                   seconds,* PRATT *lifts his head and peers
                   cautiously over the top of the settee to see*
                   DOROTHY'S *body.*)

PRATT   (*whimpering*) Thompson . . . Thompson.

                   (PRATT *succumbs to his fear and tries to
                   burrow under the cushions again as the
                   curtain falls.*)

Scene Two

*One hour later. All are assembled in the lounge with the
exception of* PRATT. MARGARET *and* ELIZABETH *are sitting on the
settee.* JOAN *is sitting on the chair down left.* PIERRE *is sitting
on the chair down right and* CHARLES *on the chair by the fire.*
BUNTING *is standing by the sideboard and* THOMKINS *is by the
hall door.* PRATT *enters from the dining room carrying a book.*

PRATT   (*looking at the cover of the book*) Very
                 interesting. Very interesting indeed.

                 (PRATT *places the book on the desk.*)

                 So . . . you all maintain that when the shots
                 were fired you were in your rooms.

CHARLES   Except for me, old boy. Just nipped outside for
                 a spot of air.

THOMKINS   And me, sir. I was in the downstairs lavatory.

PRATT   I'm aware of that, Thompson. Pity you weren't
                 out of there a bit faster.

THOMKINS   I would have been, sir, but it was rather
                 difficult. When I opened the door, the Colonel
                 was holding the gun in a firing position. I
                 thought my number was up.

PRATT   (*mystified*) What number?

THOMKINS   It's just a saying, sir.

PRATT   Mmn. Can you explain, Colonel?

CHARLES   Simple really. It's the same as . . . thought I'd
                 had it . . . had my chips.

PRATT   No, why you had the gun!

CHARLES   Oh, sorry, old chap, get you now. I rushed in,
                 spotted the gun lying there, picked it up.

THOMKINS   And that's when I saw him, sir.

PRATT   I'm quite aware of that, Thompson.

THOMKINS   Sorry, sir. Just trying to clarify the events.

PRATT   (*moving to* THOMKINS) When I want clarity, I'll
                 ask for it . . . I usually manage without.

(*As* PRATT *moves away, across in front of*
THOMKINS, *he steps on his bandaged foot.*
THOMKINS *howls and hops on the spot, holding*
his foot.)

Did you see anyone else, Colonel?

CHARLES   They were all on the stairs, with the exception
of the butler chap.

JOAN   It all happened so quickly, Inspector. Suddenly
we were all on the staircase. I remember calling
to Missus Craddock.

PRATT   Do you recall what you called when you were
calling?

JOAN   It's so difficult. I believe it was, "there's
another one gone". So tragic. And if you
hadn't mislaid the gun, Inspector.

PRATT   (*rapidly changing the subject*) You were in
your room in the basement, Butler Bumsting?

BUNTING   (*sorry for himself*) I wasn't feeling very well. I
think I must have caught something.

CHARLES   Too much drink if you ask me.

PRATT   And you didn't hear the shots?

BUNTING   I didn't hear anything, your Lordship, I must
have dropped off.

PRATT   Dropped off what?

THOMKINS   He was virtually unconscious on his bed when
I checked on him, sir.

BUNTING   I think it must be the flu. (*Looking very*
queasy.) May I be excused for a moment?

PRATT   What for?

BUNTING   It's rather urgent.

             (BUNTING *staggers quickly into the dining
             room. The telephone rings.*)

PRATT   Ah . . . that'll be the phone.

             (THOMKINS *answers the phone.*)

THOMKINS   Bagshot house, Constable Thomkins . . .
             feeling much better thank you, sir . . .
             Sergeant? . . . One moment, sir. (*To* PRATT.) It's
             for you, Sarge . . . the Deputy Chief Constable.

             (PRATT *moves nervously to the phone. In taking
             the phone and turning,* PRATT *manages to wrap
             the cord around his neck.*)

PRATT   Pratt, sir . . . I'm afraid so, sir, but it wasn't
             exactly under my nose . . . yes, same weapon,
             sir . . . immediately? But, sir . . . yes, sir . . . sir.

             (PRATT s*adly extricates himself from the cord
             and replaces the receiver.*)

THOMKINS   (*cheerily*) Didn't sound very pleased, Sarge.

PRATT   No, Thompson, he wasn't. You're going to be
             in very hot water over this. (*To the others.*)
             Right, I want to get this cleared up once and
             for all. I haven't got long, I'm wanted back at
             the station . . . another important case.

CHARLES   We won't detain you then, old boy.

PRATT   Not so fast, Colonel. There's one thing that's
             been praying on my mind. Missus Marbles, you
             said that before Miss Bogshot was shot, she
             went into the dining room, looking for a book?

JOAN   Yes, Inspector.

PRATT   Well I've taken the trouble to interrogate the
             book case. There was one book which caught

my eye, separate from the rest . . . and it's in
this book that I believe the answer to our
mystery lies.

(PRATT *moves to the desk and lifts the book
triumphantly. He reads the cover.*)

"The Art of Macrame". (*Smiling expectantly.*)
Does this mean anything to any of you?

(*There is complete silence.*)

(*disappointed*) You disappoint me. (*Flicking
through the book.*) I felt sure this book held
the key.

(*A key drops from the book, onto the floor.*)

(*surprised*) Ah . . . the key.

(PRATT *picks up the key.*)

If I'm not mistaken, this key holds the key. At a
guess I'd say it's the key to the front door.

JOAN   I believe you'll find it's a safe key, Inspector.

PRATT   But of course, Missus Marbles. Why should
                we anticipate danger from a mere key!

JOAN   No, Inspector. The key to the safe.

                (PIERRE *and* ELIZABETH *look worried.*)

PRATT   The safe? Precisely what I was thinking,
                Missus Marbles. If you'll bear with me but a
                moment, I will unlock our proverbial panda's
                box.

                (PRATT *marches proudly into the dining room,
                then returns a couple of seconds later.*)

                Where's the safe, Thompson?

THOMKINS   Don't know, Sarge.

PIERRE   (*thinking quickly*) I believe I know, Inspector. (*Moving to* PRATT *and holding out his hand.*) Per'aps you will allow me the 'onour of assisting you.

PRATT   (*flattered*) Thank you, Monsieur.

     (PIERRE *takes the key and exits to the hall.*)

THOMKINS   But, Sarge!

PRATT   Stop fussing, Thompson. Pity you don't show that sort of initiative.

JOAN   (*suddenly*) I think you'll find the contents of the safe unimportant, Inspector. I believe I know the identity of the murderer.

PRATT   You do!

JOAN   I've come across many similar cases . . . and this particular one seems to follow a typical pattern.

PRATT   (*wisely*) Quite so. Continue, Missus Marbles. I suspect that your suspicions will confirm the suspicions which I already suspect.

     (*As* JOAN *speaks,* PRATT *hurriedly scribbles notes in his notebook.*)

JOAN   I believe that Missus Bagshot had a half brother of Rumanian nationality . . . a half brother who was rejected by his family and took refuge in Albania, where he mixed with dubious company. He had an illegitimate daughter by the name of Elana. Scorned and humiliated by the family for many years, they plotted to gain revenge and inherit a fortune.

     (JOAN *pauses for effect. The others wait in eager anticipation.*)

It is my belief that Mister Bunting is that man . . . (*The others gasp.*) . . . and Elizabeth is his daughter.

ELIZABETH (*outraged*) What a ridiculous suggestion! You can't possibly believe that?

PRATT But I do. As it happens, it's a line of investigation which I also have been following. Would you care to reveal your proof, Missus Marbles?

JOAN I'm afraid that's not possible, Inspector.

PRATT Come now . . . don't be so modest.

JOAN But I have none.

PRATT What!

JOAN I was merely postulating, Inspector. Usually, upon my revelations, the murderer immediately breaks down and confesses. Unfortunately on this occasion I seem to have failed.

PRATT You mean you made it up!

JOAN Absolutely, Inspector. I thought it was worth a try.

PRATT (*furious, crossing out the notes in his notebook*) Missus Marbles, do you realise the seriousness of your rash pustule? I could have you charged with . . . with . . . with a very serious charge.

(PIERRE *enters from the hall. He carries a small wad of bank notes.*)

PIERRE I am sorry, Inspector, but I bring unfortunate news. The safe was empty except for a small amount of money . . . a trifle.

(PIERRE *hands the money to* PRATT.)

PRATT	A pity . . . I had high hopes.
	(PRATT *thumbs through the wad of notes, then places it in his pocket.*)
	I'd best hold onto this . . . could be important.
THOMKINS	(*to* PIERRE) No copy of the will I suppose?
PIERRE	Non.
PRATT	(*bored*) I think we've already covered all possibilities with the will, Thompson.
THOMKINS	But things have changed, Sarge. The Colonel now inherits the estate.
PRATT	Does he? Do you?
CHARLES	So it would seem, old boy.
MARGARET	(*stunned*) What! Charles, what are you saying?
PRATT	No doubt a surprise. But then you weren't aware of the long standing relationship between your husband and the late Miss Bogshot.
MARGARET	Relationship! With Mildred! I can assure you that my husband has had no relationships, Sergeant . . . not even with me. Tell him, Charles.
CHARLES	(*sadly*) 'Fraid I can't, old girl. It's true.
MARGARET	Don't, Charles. Stop it now!
CHARLES	This is really too much, Sergeant. I gave you information in the strictest confidence.
PRATT	Regrettable but inevitable. Another crime has been perpetuated. Over a great many years

your husband had a lustful, sinful, pestilent affair with Miss Bogshot. As a token of her esteem, she made certain provisions in her will. With the death of Missus Foxhole, Colonel Codling becomes major beneficiary.

MARGARET   (*sobbing*) How could you do it, Charles? How could you do it to me?

PRATT   I think that concludes the investigation.

THOMKINS   Are you sure, Sarge?

PRATT   No doubt, Thompson. (*Pompously pointing at* CHARLES.) Major Beneficiary came here with the express intent of killing the two ladies of the house. He did so with ruthless cunning, expecting to outwit the forces of the law. Unfortunately for him, he didn't count on me.

(*On his final line,* PRATT *attempts to pose by leaning casually against the back of the settee. He misses it and falls out of sight behind the settee. He leaps to his feet, pretending nothing has happened.*)

CHARLES   This is preposterous!

PRATT   I think not. You were close to the scene of the crime on both occasions. Just before Miss Bogshot was shot she said, "so you've found". As I deducted at the time, she was about to say "your gun". The gun which you were holding.

THOMKINS   Actually, I deduced it, Sarge.

PRATT   Stop trying to be clever, Thompson. Missus Foxhole's last words were, "he's trying to kill me" . . . *he*. You again, Major. Neither Butler Bumsting nor Mister Marseillaise had anything to gain by killing her. Charge him, Thompson.

(THOMKINS *takes* CHARLES *by the arm and leads him to the window.* THOMKINS *takes out a*

notebook and starts to talk quietly to
CHARLES.)

You accused me of incompetence, Major . . .
were the first to cast nasturtiums against me.
(*Smiling smugly.*) Perhaps now you see how
incompetent I really am.

MARGARET   (*quietly*) My husband may be an adulterer, but
you're very wrong about one thing, Sergeant.

PRATT   I think not. I'm rarely really wrong.

MARGARET   My husband wasn't the only man with a motive
for killing Dorothy. Ask Pierre . . . or perhaps I
should say Peter. When my husband was
phoning your superior, I came downstairs. I
overheard Pierre and Elizabeth talking about
Dorothy. She had some kind of evidence
against them. They were planning to kill her.

PIERRE   What a ridiculous suggestion. 'Ow can you
think of such a thing!

ELIZABETH   You can't possibly believe her, Inspector. The
poor woman's obviously deranged . . . it must
be the shock. She's trying to protect her
husband.

MARGARET   And you need not continue with those phoney
accents. He's no more French than you are,
Sergeant, and she's a common slut.

ELIZABETH   I will not stay and listen to this nonsense any
longer!

(ELIZABETH *rises and moves to the hall door.*)

THOMKINS   Just a moment, Miss. I think these two may
have some explaining to do, Sarge.

JOAN   I think I may be able to help, Inspector. I
remember now . . . Mildred seemed rather

concerned . . . something to do with these paintings.

CHARLES   Not real paintings of course . . . copies. (*Pointing to* PIERRE.) He supplied them.

MARGARET   They're in it together.

PRATT   So, the thick plottens yet again. What are your real and proper names?

ELIZABETH   Don't say anything, Pierre. This is all a ghastly misunderstanding.

PIERRE   (*in his real voice*) It's no use, Elizabeth.

ELIZABETH   Pierre . . . Please!

PIERRE   The game's up, Elizabeth, can't you see?

ELIZABETH   (*in her real voice*) Fool! Well you're not 'aving me!

            (ELIZABETH *runs for the hall door.*)

PRATT   Grab her, Thompson!

            (THOMKINS *tries to hold* ELIZABETH *but she stamps on his bandaged foot and he hops away, howling. He falls into the chair by the fire.* ELIZABETH *opens the door to the hall and tries to rush out, but she rebounds off* BUNTING *who is just entering.* CHARLES *grabs hold of* ELIZABETH.)

ELIZABETH   Let go! You can't prove a thing.

CHARLES   Well done, Bunting, old chap. Arrived in the nick of time!

            (BUNTING *looks confused, then queasy. He exits rapidly down the hall.*)

            Bit like the old Keystone Cops eh, Sergeant?

(THOMKINS *is still incapacitated on the chair.*)

PRATT   Hold on to her, Major. Pull yourself together,
        Thompson. You were saying, Mister
        Marseillaise?

PIERRE Elizabeth and I were working together. Two
        years ago we sold these paintings to Missus
        Bagshot . . . except before dispatch we
        swapped the originals for these copies.
        Dorothy found out. She tried to blackmail us.

PRATT   So you mortally killed her.

PIERRE I didn't . . . we didn't. We haven't killed
        anyone!

PRATT   I think that's for me to decide.

CHARLES I told Mildred these were copies. Blighter must
        have overheard.

PRATT   You incurably murdered them both to save
        your own skins. As I suspected from the start.

PIERRE We haven't hurt anyone!

PRATT   I don't think that will wear in a court of legal
        law. You should be more careful. You know
        what put me on to you? When you returned
        and claimed that there was a trifle in the safe . .
        . the ramblings of a mad man. (*Proudly.*) And
        so I conclude my conclusions. A classically
        conducted investigation of a case which will be
        recorded in the annals of most criminal crime . .
        . the two young innocents . . . murdered to
        death. Take him out, Thompson . . . I'll man-
        handle Miss Hardly-Trumping.

        (THOMKINS *escorts* PIERRE *into the hall.* PRATT
        follows with ELIZABETH.)

        Good afternoon all.

JOAN How shocking. They seemed such fine young
people. It never fails to amaze me . . . the
depths to which the human spirit will sink.

CHARLES Knew the fellow looked suspicious. Spot 'em a
mile off.

MARGARET (*sharply*) I shall instruct Bunting to fetch my
bags downstairs.

(MARGARET *moves quickly to the hall, ignoring
the pleas of* CHARLES.)

CHARLES Wait a minute, old girl, I can explain. (*Sadly to*
JOAN.) Don't suppose she'll want to listen.

JOAN I think you should give her time, Colonel. Time
is a great healer of wounds, physical or mental.

CHARLES She's never been one for patience. Hard to
explain to a woman how a chap feels. Dashed
awkward. Pity women aren't a bit more like
chaps . . . make life a lot simpler.

JOAN I expect you could stay here for the moment,
Colonel. After all, this will all belong to you.

CHARLES Can't even think about it at the moment. Too
damned confused. Own fault . . . shouldn't
have carried on with Mildred . . . bad form.

JOAN You mustn't be too harsh on yourself, Colonel.
We all have our weaknesses . . . affairs . . . the
sensuous curve of a young girls breast . . . the
half glimpse of a virgin's thigh.

(MARGARET *enters from the hall.*)

MARGARET I'm taking the car, Charles. You may make your
own arrangements. I'll have your things
delivered to the club. You'll be hearing from my
solicitor.

(MARGARET *turns to exit*.)

CHARLES — Just a moment, Margaret. No need to go off in a huff like this. Sit down . . . we can have a bit of a chin wag.

MARGARET — There is nothing to discuss.

CHARLES — Look, old girl . . .

MARGARET — (*venomous, closing the hall door and turning on* CHARLES) Don't you dare old girl me! Thirty five years we've been married, Charles, and from day one it's been old girl this and old girl that!

CHARLES — Never realised it upset you, old girl . . . sorry.

MARGARET — There are a lot of things you never realised, Charles. You were too busy making up your pathetic stories . . . too busy at the club, trying to impress your friends. Too busy to notice me!

CHARLES — But you didn't complain . . . too much. Thought you were reasonably content.

MARGARET — Content! God, I don't know what Mildred saw in you. Or were you different with her!

CHARLES — Don't think so.

MARGARET — I've been trapped, Charles. There was no way out . . . not until now. Do you realise that you're suddenly very wealthy, Charles? I'm going to squeeze every last penny out of you. What do you say to that?

CHARLES — You seem a spot upset, old girl.

MARGARET — You're pathetic, Charles . . . pathetic.

CHARLES — But I'll make it up to you. Scouts honour and all that. Don't know where I'd be without you.

MARGARET   It's too late for that . . . much too late. I've got
                everything I came here for!

                (MARGARET *realises that she has said too*
                much. She moves towards the door.)

CHARLES   What do you mean? Got everything you came
                for?

MARGARET   That's not important.

                (MARGARET *moves towards the door again, but*
                CHARLES *blocks her path.*)

CHARLES   What do you mean!

JOAN   You knew about Mildred and your husband
                before you came here.

MARGARET   That's no concern of yours. It makes no
                difference now.

JOAN   And I suspect you knew about the will.

MARGARET   So what if I did!

JOAN   I've been very stupid. If you overheard
                Elizabeth and Pierre planning to kill Dorothy,
                why didn't you say something straight away?
                You wanted her dead.

MARGARET   Oh, you're very clever. Yes I wanted her dead .
                . . but I didn't kill her.

JOAN   But you killed Mildred. That's what she was
                trying to say . . . "so you've found your
                husband's gun".

CHARLES   That's quite enough. Can't be true. Margaret
                wouldn't be capable of harming anyone . . . she
                wouldn't know how.

MARGARET   Even now you underestimate me.

CHARLES   Margaret, you don't know what you're saying!

MARGARET   Oh yes I do. (*Proudly.*) Yes, I did kill Mildred.

CHARLES   No!

MARGARET   That shocks you? Good. I found out about you and Mildred . . . from one of your so-called friends at the club. He even passed on some of her letters. I found out about the will. Suddenly it was my big chance. I could divorce a wealthy man.

CHARLES   But the estate was left to Dorothy.

MARGARET   Unfortunately I only got half the story. I didn't discover that part until we arrived here.

JOAN   So then you realised that Dorothy had to die.

MARGARET   Quite. I was going to leave it for a respectable time. Then I had a stroke of luck. I overheard Elizabeth and Pierre. It was perfect. All I had to do was sit and wait.

JOAN   And they killed her for you.

MARGARET   I'm afraid you're not quite as clever as you thought, Miss Maple. They didn't kill her.

JOAN   But it wasn't you. She said, "*he's* trying to kill me".

MARGARET   And so he was.

JOAN   Who?

(BUNTING *enters from the hall. He carries the gun menacingly and grins inanely. He stands just inside the doorway, closing the door behind him.*)

BUNTING   Me.

ACT TWO

(JOAN *and* CHARLES *spin round to look at him.*)

JOAN   Mister Bunting . . . but why?

MARGARET   Charles was quite right. He had seen Robert somewhere before . . . in my bed.

CHARLES   Bunting? But it's not Bunting is it . . . it's Benson . . . mess orderly. You ran off the same night with the mess silver!

BUNTING   That's right.

CHARLES   Baggy Bob Benson . . . that's what we used to call him. But that was over twenty years ago!

MARGARET   Twenty eight to be exact, Charles. My one moment of excitement in a dreary marriage. I recognised Robert as soon as I arrived here . . . it was very convenient. He was quite happy to help me for a proportion of the profits. After I shot Mildred he took me into the cellar and up the back stairs.

JOAN   But I don't understand why he killed Dorothy . . . someone else was going to do it for you.

MARGARET   Robert almost bungled that. When I explained to him that Dorothy was to be killed, he was too drunk to understand. He thought he had to do it. He poked his head from the basement, shot her and then feigned unconsciousness. We were lucky to get away with that.

JOAN   But you haven't, my dear. We know all about it now.

(JOAN *walks confidently to the phone.*)

BUNTING   (*threatening*) Get away from that.

(JOAN *hesitates.*)

MARGARET   (*pleasantly*) We'll have to arrange a little adventure for you both. A tragic accident. Over the cliff in the car I think.

CHARLES   Oh no, not the Bentley!

MARGARET   A little embarrassing, coming so soon after the other killings, but then, the police already have the murderers. And it does have advantages . . . we get all the money.

CHARLES   You can't mean it, old girl.

MARGARET   Just watch me. Keep them covered, Robert.

(BUNTING *waves the gun threateningly as* PRATT *suddenly opens the hall door and takes a step inside. He sees* BUNTING *holding the gun and takes it from him. They all stand motionless in surprised silence.*)

PRATT   Thank you, Mister Bumsting. I wondered where Thompson had left it. Good afternoon all.

(PRATT *raises his hat politely and exits to the hall, closing the door behind him. There is a moments silence before* JOAN *recovers her senses.*)

JOAN   (*shouting*) Inspector . . . help. You've got the wrong ones. Inspector . . .

(PRATT *pokes his head back around the door.*)

PRATT   Pardon?

(*There is sudden chaos.* BUNTING *gives* PRATT *a sharp chop to the back of the neck.* PRATT *drops, pole-axed and* BUNTING *runs over him and out into the hall.* CHARLES *tries to grab* MARGARET, *but she kicks his shin and he lets her go.* MARGARET *runs to the door, arriving just as* PRATT *is trying to get to his knees. She pushes him down again and runs over him and into the hall.* PRATT *gets to his feet, stunned and confused.*)

JOAN   Stop them, Inspector . . . they're the murderers!

PRATT   What . . . oh, right.

(*In his confusion,* PRATT *moves towards the dining room, waving the gun.*)

JOAN   Not there, Inspector . . . outside!

PRATT   Ah.

(PRATT *moves to the window and shouts.*)

Stop them, Thompson . . . come on, man, you can hop faster than that! Right . . . out of the way, man.

(PRATT *smashes the window with the gun and tries to take careful aim. He is hopeless and, in the end, covers his eyes with one hand, turns his head away from the gun and fires blindly. There is a muffled cry from outside.* PRATT *uncovers his eyes, looking pleased and surprised. He peers out of the window before turning back into the room with a satisfied smile. With sudden realisation and horror, he rushes back to look through the window. He finally moves, sad, defeated and broken, back into the room.*)

PRATT   I wonder if one of you might assist Constable Thompson. He appears to have damaged his other foot.

(*Blackout.*)

FURNITURE AND PROPERTY LIST

ACT ONE

Scene One

Set: Sideboard with 1930s style telephone
                Writing desk with trick "breakable ornament".
                Table with lamp and Mildred's spectacles
                Settee with scatter cushions
                Four chairs
                Coffee table with magazines
                Two paintings over fireplace
                Wooden elephant and coal scuttle on hearth
                Fire effect in fireplace

Offstage: Log, axe (BUNTING)
                Silver tray with sherry decanter and glasses
                (DOROTHY)
                Revolver and white gloves

Personal: White gloves (BUNTING)
                White gloves (ELIZABETH)

Scene Two

Strike: Used glasses

Set: Bottle of sherry and glasses on sideboard

Offstage: Plate of teacakes, spread with jam (JOAN)
                Revolver (THOMKINS)

Personal: Knitting (JOAN)
                Notebook and pencil (PRATT)
                Notebook and pencil (THOMKINS)

ACT TWO

Scene One

Strike: Plate with teacakes

Set: Sherry decanter and glasses on sideboard

Offstage: Brandy bottle (BUNTING)
                Walking stick (THOMKINS)

Personal: Handbag containing handkerchief (DOROTHY)

Scene Two

Strike: Used glasses

Offstage: Book with key inside (PRATT)
                Small wad of bank notes (PIERRE)
                Revolver (BUNTING)

Personal: Notebook and pencil (THOMKINS)

LIGHTING PLOT

Act One

Scene One:

Interior: Artificial light
                Fire effect in fireplace

Exterior: Dusk

All Other Scenes:

Interior: Natural light
                Fire effect in fireplace

Exterior: Day

SOUND AND VISUAL EFFECTS PLOT
ACT ONE
Scene One

Cue 1:   MILDRED: ". . . who would want him!"
                Page 6: Door bell rings.

Cue 2:   CHARLES: ". . . came across a lot in India y'know"
                Page 15: Door bell rings.

Cue 3:   DOROTHY: "Oh . . . what a pity"
                Page 26: Door bell rings.

Cue 4:   MILDRED: "Bunting, really!"
                Page 27: Door bell rings.

Cue 5:   MILDRED: ". . . So you've found . . ."
                Page 33: Shot from revolver in hall doorway.

Scene Two

Cue 6:   THOMKINS: ". . . So you've found . . ."
                Page 58: Revolver shot as Pratt fires.

ACT TWO
Scene One

Cue 7:   DOROTHY: "I need to speak to you, Inspector"
                Page 72: Telephone rings.

Cue 8:   PRATT: "Coming Thompson, ready or not"
                Page 82: Two revolver shots followed by a scream
                from Dorothy (off in hall).

Cue 9:   DOROTHY: "He's trying to kill . . ."
                Page 82: Shot from revolver (off in hall).

Scene Two

Cue 10:   BUNTING: "It's rather urgent"
                Page 85: Telephone rings.

Cue 11:   PRATT: ". . . out of the way, man"
                Page 100: Sound of breaking glass as Pratt
                "smashes" the window; Revolver shot as Pratt
                fires.

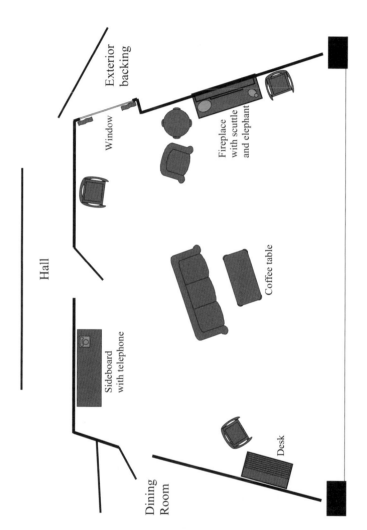

Murdered to Death - Set